Copyright © 2016

Published by:
New Year Publishing, LLC
144 Diablo Ranch Court
Danville, CA 94506 USA

http://www.newyearpublishing.com

ISBN 978-1-61431-062-4

*This book is dedicated to my five children, Brittany, Sebastian, India, Rhys, Portia; to my father who is always there with me; to the love of my life, Cassandra Owens; and to my co-founders Neehar Giri and Kent Perkocha for taking this ridiculously incredible journey with me.*

# Acknowledgements

I would like to thank and acknowledge all the amazing Apttus customers, partners and employees.

I would also like to thank those that helped make this book possible including Jeff Cowan, Zack Alspaugh, Alex Cohen, Daniel Louie, Adina Crossley, Ben Allen, Kamal Ahluwalia, Michael Dunne, Fady Stephanos, Stephen Kretchman, Sean Joyce, Brion Schwers, Elliott Yama, Louis Columbus, Stephanie Tilton, and Maria Pergolino.

# Contents

# A Note to Visionary Business Leaders

*"Any intelligent fool can make things bigger and more complex.
It takes a touch of genius and a lot of courage to move in
the opposite direction."*
*– Albert Einstein –*

In 2006, after having worked 15 years for software companies and observing the "not so good" customer experience, I had several groundbreaking realizations that began to shape my thinking about the value that a software package provides to customers. My first observation was that automating a business process, using a software package, is a good thing, but doesn't necessarily provide the business outcome that you seek. Second, that arguably the most important business process in your company—the Quote-to-Cash process—the process that defines the revenue of your company, is shockingly "unautomated," manual and fraught with risk. Corporations have essentially automated almost every other process in their companies. But the one that matters most for revenue, has been neglected. And third, the realization that there is a unique moment in time in the company's lifecycle, that when managed to maximum effect, can materially change the revenue of your company. And that moment is when pricing is first offered to a potential customer, either by your salesperson, a website, or another channel. At that point in time, you are defining the revenue for your company.

How do these observations all come together?

1

Firstly, automating the Quote-to-Cash process by itself is not good enough. Other elements must come together to ensure that you actually realize the business outcome. At any particular step in the Quote-to-Cash process, the person involved should also have incentives to change behavior to affect the outcome you want. Traditionally, process automation applications do not have behavior based applications "wrapped" around them. These applications need to be incorporated into Quote-to-Cash automation in order to ensure behavior change. Additionally, equipping your users with other information or intelligent insights, can also radically change your outcome to what you want. Enterprise Application providers typically don't think of these three genres of applications all coming together and they usually only provide one genre of applications. Therefore, outcomes are not maximized.

When a price is offered to a customer, the revenue for your company is being determined. And amazingly, in my experiences, I found that most companies are creating and delivering quotes using spreadsheets, rudimentary systems, emails and many disparate customer engagement tools. In other words, companies are severely neglecting the moment that defines their revenue!

Why wouldn't you put absolutely everything your organization has to bear at that moment in time in order to ensure that you are absolutely maximizing your revenue? Why wouldn't you equip your employees with a smart quoting tool? Why wouldn't you align the compensation of your salespeople to the discounts or other parameters of the quote? Why wouldn't you call upon other insights or learnings from the rest of the company that could provide intelligence at that critical point in time when a quote is being presented to a customer? There is so much that can be done to maximize the moment that defines the revenue for your company.

Amazingly, this is not happening. So I got together with two friends to start Apttus, a Quote-to-Cash software provider with a vision to fix all of this. To empower companies to not just automate the Quote-to-Cash process, but to apply everything possible at the moment of defining revenue for your company. Apttus has achieved extraordinary success and it's all due to our customers who understood this concept and elected to take the journey with Apttus.

At the beginning of our journey, we recognized that the management of contracts are a very important part of the success of an organization, and are the lifeblood of every business. But we saw that organizations across industries were manually pulling data into a contract from a variety of sources to represent a mix of products, prices, terms, and other contractual details. We also saw that organizations faced similar challenges when it came to billing and invoicing, quoting, deal management and in fact all elements of the Quote-to-Cash process. In other words, from the start of a customer engagement until the time companies recognize revenues, they are trying to manually solve the up-front complexity associated with selling effectively and with little assistance.

Streamlining and automating Quote-to-Cash helps companies generate more revenue, and makes your company "easy to do business with" while reducing risk and increasing sales efficiency. This is a necessity in a world where companies—enabled by the digitalization of business and the rise of cloud applications—are moving to accommodating customer needs, increasing selling through new channels and adapting to new business models. To be successful, we need to face this daunting reality head on.

Usually people in Sales, Sales Operations, Marketing, Legal, Finance, Operations, IT, or any management position, share a common goal: to make customers happy and to drive more revenue for their company. Yet amazingly, they are still hamstrung by one of the most painstakingly manual processes in their business: the Quote-to-Cash process. The Quote-to-Cash business process connects a customer's intent to buy with the fulfillment of the order and the company's realization of revenue—and is *the* revenue process of a company.

Because the Quote-to-Cash process is at the heart of every company's ability to drive revenue, manage risk, and more importantly, drive customer satisfaction, it is arguably the most important process for businesses to master. Yet as I have described, it's also one of the most poorly implemented business processes, executed across an array of siloed departments and platforms and riddled with manual steps.

Addressing this problem is actually one of the most pressing issues facing businesses today. PWC recently published a report stating, "Quote-to-Cash processes touch almost every function within the organization—sales, finance, IT, R&D, marketing, legal, supply chain, order management and customer service—and are integral to successful channel partner relationships. As a result, improving Quote-to-Cash operations has a potentially profound effect across both the front and back office."[1]

It's long been a truism that companies failing to eliminate manual processes, fall behind. But in today's digital-first world, companies that fail to automate and streamline electronic processes, are at an even greater risk of being bypassed more than ever before.

Why hasn't true automation of Quote-to-Cash taken place in most companies? Because the "market" was conditioned to believe that you automate one process step at a time: you automate contracts, or you automate quotes, or billing etc. As a result, a dizzying array of software providers came to market, each only offering a package for their respective step in the Quote-to-Cash process. Software providers that only manage quoting, or only contracts, or only billing popped up over the last 10 years. But *no one* was offering an end-to-end Quote-to-Cash solution addressing the true business problem.

The answer isn't to automate individual processes such as quoting, contract management, billing and invoicing, but to focus on the process at large. So as companies began to automate these individual process steps, they were actually exacerbating the problem of siloed systems! And even more ironic, by automating these elements, companies were simply pushing these siloed, discrete systems to the

---

[1] PWC, Technology industry at the cross-roads: Transforming quote-to-cash operations, 2013

cloud—not solving the overall problem at all. Although the cloud is a very powerful way of getting value from enterprise applications, pushing to the cloud itself is not solving the issue. Without an integrated, end-to-end Quote-to-Cash system, they couldn't address the actual problem of not having a single view of a customer, transaction or order.

As I had mentioned previously, while enterprise applications exist to automate a process, they traditionally have not focused on actually changing the business outcome. Software companies are focused on competing on a feature-function level, as opposed to focusing on achieving the business outcome for the customer. For example, while a Configure Price Quote (CPQ) application streamlines the process of submitting a quote for approval, in most cases, the approver lacks all needed information to properly evaluate the quote. As a result, the quote gets approved anyway, just as it would have via the manual process—nothing really changed. The outcome is the same.

The real goal of an enterprise application should be to achieve the business outcome that the customer is seeking. This requires not just providing functionality to automate the process, but also functionality to influence the user's behavior to achieve the most favorable outcome possible for your company.

Secondly, you need to automate the end-to-end Quote-to-Cash process—connecting all the dots across disjointed departments and systems—and then adding a layer of intelligence and guidance. We call this *Intelligent* Quote to Cash. This a-ha moment triggered us to develop a vision of how organizations should manage their entire revenue operation. As we formulated our vision, we focused on how to enable every successful company to tap into the behavior of their top talent in their organizations, expertise of their best sales reps, strongest product experts, top financial analysts etc. In a sense, to bring their company's dream team into every deal by using artificial intelligence technologies that provide insights to users. Our goal was to empower everyone to create, manage and close deals like those that do it best—to maximize revenue.

Inspired by this idea, we began our journey by changing the conversation with our prospects from talking about what features and functions they needed, to what matters most—the business outcome. We then realized we were truly pioneering the Quote-to-Cash space and, through hundreds of customer engagements, collected an enormous amount of information on best practices, methods, and ideas and decided we would share this with the world at large. These learnings have become the basis of this book.

Based on hundreds of customer engagements, we've identified essentially nine business outcomes that typically help companies address the most common process-related challenges:

- Improved accuracy
- Faster time to market
- More simplicity
- Higher sales effectiveness
- Higher sales efficiency
- Bigger deal size
- More opportunities
- Higher win rates
- Improved margins

And as we identified these outcomes and began to recast the conversation with our customers, we began to achieve significant benefits for our customers—more than they had ever imagined.

Also, we continually called upon the philosophy espoused by one of my childhood idols, Reinhold Messner. This incredible freestyle mountain climber shocked the world when he solo climbed Mt. Everest in 1980 without supplemental oxygen for the first time in the history of mankind. He went on to climb the other 13 tallest peaks in the world the same way, and he became known as having "defied gravity" because he achieved the unthinkable. And he achieved this because of three things in his mind:

- Not listen to conventional thinking
- Fearing nothing
- Believing in yourself

I mention this here because we know how intimidating it was for us to start our own software company in order to make large, fundamental changes with our customers. And we know how hard it is to consider making a major change of this type to get your business modernized for Quote-to-Cash. But it can be done. And when done right, will provide amazing benefits. Follow these philosophies and you can easily modernize your Quote-to-Cash process. And then you'll be considered a hero for having spearheaded the change that tremendously benefited your organization.

Now is the time to break away from the historical, linear process-oriented approach and embrace an outcome-based, behavior-driven and machine-intelligent strategy. Now is the time to step up and lead your company down the path to a smarter Quote-to-Cash process. Do so and you'll drive better business results than you could ever imagine. Companies that have truly automated the end-to-end Intelligent Quote-to-Cash process have on average realized 105% larger deal sizes, 28% shorter sales cycles, and 26% more reps achieving quota. In fact, Nucleus Research found that Quote-to-Cash applications can deliver 4.2 times the ROI of traditional core customer relationship management applications.[1]

No one may have asked you to fix your Quote-to-Cash process—but it's one area of your business that affects all others. And people across your organization will certainly see the benefit when you knock down the current barriers that are preventing your company from achieving its full potential. When cross-functional teams are empowered to work together to achieve a common goal, they are more engaged, more efficient, and more productive. And when companies harness

---

[1] Nucleus Research, EDGE CRM DELIVERS 4.2 TIMES MORE ROI, 2016

the true and full potential of their employees, they can do amazing things. At the end of the day, deciding to go in this direction is about deciding to defy gravity—but doing so with the right tools to succeed.

This book provides the foundation you need in order to dramatically improve your Quote-to-Cash process. Using the concepts in this book and by automating the process with an intelligent, outcome-based approach, you will transform your organization. Let's explore how you can lead the charge for true and meaningful business change!

*Kirk Krappe, CEO and co-founder of Apttus*

# 1 The World in Transformation
## It's No Longer Business as Usual

Enterprises today face a business climate that is much more fluid, fast changing and challenging than ever before. And more often than not, enterprises are largely unprepared for this new normal. Siloed departments, entrenched custom-built systems and disjointed processes hold back an organization. All this inhibits the ability to respond to real customer demands and rapidly changing marketplaces. Add to that, organizational pressures to adopt to new, fast-moving technologies like social media, mobile applications and virtual reality, along with rising customer expectations to be serviced in pseudo real time. It all points to the need for a complete and fundamental change in the way you engage with your customers—or you will lose business to those who embrace this new reality and provide better service to *your* customers.

These disconnects across business processes today prevent organizations from reaching their full potential and make it difficult to create value and generate returns. Many times these disconnects can lead to major issues that threaten a company's very existence.

---

*"Businessmen go down with their business because they like the old way so well they cannot bring themselves to change..."*
*- Henry Ford -*

---

But the world is intelligent today—companies can leverage so many best practices and deep experiences, and many have done so in taking steps to modernize different areas of their businesses. In the past few decades, the focus has been on ERP and CRM automation. Automating these areas is critical to enable systems of record for financial data and customer data and, theoretically, single views of the same data. But the irony is that the process that connects these two systems—Quote-to-Cash—remains fragmented, disjointed, and most times almost completely manual. For many companies this has now become a very limiting factor to address the new world pressures.

Quote-to-Cash is the vital business process between the buyer's interest in a purchase and the company's realization of revenue, and it encompasses the entirety of a company's sales, contract, ordering, billing and customer relationship lifecycles.

Arguably Quote-to-Cash is the most important business process in your company. It is the process that generates revenue and yet typically remains unintegrated and unautomated! Even though the data captured in this process is highly relevant when it comes to quotes, contracts and revenue management, it is kept siloed and manually managed. This introduces all sorts of complications and failures in the business. Each department uses an array of disjointed systems and platforms to handle these functions in separate processes riddled with manual, disconnected steps and outdated concepts.

In fact, many companies manage this vital process using nothing more than desktop productivity tools such as Microsoft Office spreadsheets and documents.

But why does this matter? Because the Quote-to-Cash process determines your company's revenue. At the moment in time that a prospective customer receives a quote, your company's revenue is being determined. From that point onwards, the revenue your company will achieve is either what is reflected in the quote or lower if the price gets negotiated. Rarely does it go up! So in fact, maximum revenue potential for your company happens at the time of quoting to your customer. And if the quote is not optimized or maximized, your revenue will only go down from there. It is probably the single most important inflection point in your organization that affects a business outcome. That means it's imperative to bring to bear absolutely everything possible and have a major focus on this small step in the overall Quote-to-Cash process. No other business process makes a bigger impact on your revenue than Quote-to-Cash.

And maximizing that impact only gets more difficult if your company is selling multiple products and services. For example, offering and selling combinations of products and services in the right combinations can become very complex and difficult to determine. What is the best combination? Achieving the most value from these products and services requires you to communicate this value to partners and customers. It also means working through different pricing, terms and conditions, and finalizing contracts for each sale. It means developing the best approaches to service products, enforce service and warranty commitments, and upsell and cross-sell to customers. It essentially means you need to excel around everything that determines what your company is proposing and offering to the customer. The revenue decisions for the company are being made right here, whether you know it or not. Getting this right is imperative to the financial outcome of the enterprise.

The Quote-to-Cash business process can be simple or complex and comprises very important sub-business activities:

- Product selection, configuration and quote creation
- Pricing (including setting prices and policies on discounts)
- Generating, negotiating and signing contracts
- Contract obligation and financial management: rebates and promotions
- Billing and invoicing
- Order management: ensuring the correct order is being processed
- Revenue analysis

A flexible, end-to-end Quote-to-Cash process is a must-have in today's business world. Because Quote-to-Cash is a foundational, cross-functional process, it affects many across the organization comprising the revenue team: Sales, Sales Operations, Legal, Finance, Services, Delivery and usually the CFO. Without flexibility, your business can be materially affected: for example, missing major cross-sell and up-sell opportunities, being blind to revenue leakage, missing renewals, experiencing compliance risks or even failing to accurately capture revenues. Get it right and the business will achieve higher success, with a Quote-to-Cash system acting as a powerful engine that actually enables faster sales cycles and drives growth and cost savings. Mastering this process will enable you to understand and capitalize on market dynamics, guide salespeople and partners to sell more intelligently, outsell competitors, and raise your performance in the marketplace overall. In other words, Quote-to-Cash executed well will transform your business.

How can a business stuck with such entrenched inflexibility possibly evolve to achieve new levels of success? Especially in a rapidly changing world that gets more and more complex for businesses operating nationally and globally. Today's enterprises are being forced to navigate and manage a number of complexities:

- A proliferation of sales channels and customer-touch technologies
- Increased demand for mass customization
- Rapidly evolving business and pricing models
- More global competition and commoditization
- Rising market volatility
- Increasing regulations

Let's explore this a little more to understand how it further drives the need for an integrated Quote-to-Cash process.

## Managing more and increasingly complex channels

B2B companies have had to adapt in the digital era characterized by innovative business models and consumer-facing brands that have raised the bar on customer experience and disaggregation. Today's buyers want a combination of products and services, and even "digital goods," and expect to access them in the most convenient and cost effective way possible, whether direct, online, through a distributor, another third party, through a mobile device, or via social media.

In fact, according to Forrester, "B2B buyers today not only prefer to research online, but they also prefer to buy online. Nearly 75% indicate that buying from a website is more convenient than buying from a sales representative when purchasing products or services for work. In addition, 93% of B2B buyers say that they prefer to buy online rather than from a salesperson when they've decided what to buy and just need to make the purchase. Furthermore, an ever-increasing number of B2B buyers are deciding what to buy online long before they ever contact a company's salesperson, if they ever do."[1]

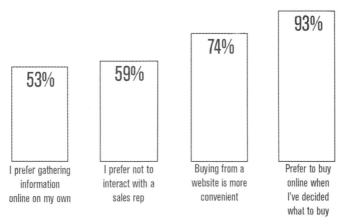

Base: 224 US B2B buyers and sellers

---

[1] Source: Forrester, *Death of A (B2B) Salesman* by Andy Hoar, April 13, 2015

The rising importance of omni-channel sales is unsurprising since E-Commerce has disrupted consumer markets for some time now—think of Circuit City and Blockbuster going out of business, or Best Buy having to confront the phenomenon of show-rooming. These same trends are now impacting the B2B world. According to Forrester, "93% of B2B buyers say that they prefer to buy online rather than from a salesperson when they've decided on what to buy."[1]

As a result, most enterprises find themselves supporting both direct and indirect channels. The direct channels often include E-Commerce and mobile options along with call center-based sales and the conventional field sales force. The indirect channels can include distributors, agents, OEMs, brokers, dealers, agents, and resellers, to name a few.

At the same time, marketplaces that were too early to the party in fifteen years ago are making a comeback. Today's technology enables companies to set up platforms that connect partners, clients and other affiliates so they can buy and sell in one electronic "location."

Now every channel has become more critical than ever before, making it imperative for companies to craft and effectively execute modern omni-channel strategies.

## Increased demand for mass customization

Just as in the consumer market, the "have it your way" culture has permeated business-to-business (B2B) markets.

The B2B space has always dealt with complex products and services requiring some level of configuration. The traditional approach has been for potential customers to engage the direct sales force and

---

[1]   Source: Forrester, *Death of A (B2B) Salesman* by Andy Hoar, April 13, 2015

spend a significant amount of time assessing and evaluating potential solutions. But as mentioned above, the digital era is driving buyers to conduct more research and place more orders online. As a result, companies that sell complex products and services must enable buyers to configure a solution based on their needs rather than on their knowledge of your products. This requires the ability to provide guided selling capabilities and advanced machine learning or artificial intelligence technologies.

In other words, your quoting solution must be embedded in each of the channels you present to your customers.

On the other side of the spectrum are B2B products that have traditionally been sold as preconfigured items or SKUs. However, since B2B buyers are also B2C consumers, they have become used to the idea of mass customization and now expect the same options in their business lives. This has left companies contending with a SKU proliferation problem and delays in the sales cycle as they attempt to accommodate the ever- changing needs of their buyers. Or they must consider deploying a quoting solution that provides them with the flexibility required to mix and match features and options to satisfy the needs of their customers.

## Setting the standard for smarter B2B buying

Just as it disrupted the consumer marketplace, Amazon is now setting the bar for how businesses should sell with its Amazon Business subsidiary. Amazon Business is a marketplace providing B2B buyers with easy access to hundreds of millions of products—everything from IT and lab equipment to education and food service supplies. In other words, it brings the selection and convenience of personal shopping online to the business world. With built-in approval workflows, the marketplace enables buyers to distribute the purchasing process across their organizations while running final purchases through a single department.

In an interview with Forrester, Dan Park, Product Management Group, and Ken Stanick, Director of Sales, Marketing and Channels for Amazon Business summarized the key themes of smarter buying:

- Help visitors find items quickly
- De-clutter screen navigation
- Showcase key categories
- Put information at fingertips
- Make it easy to compare multiple offerings

It's no wonder Gartner is encouraging businesses to "Simplify processes for accepting orders from new customers to match the simplicity at Amazon Business and compare the features provided to buyers on Amazon Business (like approval workflows) with their own offerings to develop feature parity where possible."[1]

---

[1]  Gartner, Amazon Business Offers New Opportunities for B2B Buyers — and Potential Challenges for Sellers, July 28, 2015

## Satisfying demands for flexible pricing and consumption

Spoiled by their consumer experiences, today's business customers also want the flexibility to *consume and use* solutions as fits their needs. For example, in addition to owning a product, they may want the option to subscribe and pay for actual usage.

To adapt, businesses have had to embrace, create and support new business models as the world has hurtled into subscription-based models. This has impacted every step of the order delivery process from order to cash, and every department from Sales and Finance to Legal and Operations. Moreover, it has affected a slew of business strategies and activities: pricing, packaging, promotion, sales forecasting, incentives (e.g., rebates, discounts, free trials, bundling), order fulfillment/distribution, quoting, contracts, accounts payable, revenue tracking and reconciliation. To accommodate new business models, products and services, distribution routes, and more, companies must often enable multiple transaction types, including demonstrations, freemium, volume purchase agreements, and subscriptions.

Let's isolate pricing for a moment to get a better sense of the complexity facing most businesses today.

The perfect price for a product is influenced by a variety of factors, including market demand, competitive pressures, business strategy, timing, and costs. Accounting for these constantly in-flux variables makes pricing a challenge. Businesses need the flexibility to make frequent, controlled, changes to their pricing strategy to stay with or ahead of the market.

And it's critical that companies price products and services with market conditions, prospect and buyer demographics, close rates, geography-based factors, and pricing history in mind. By doing so, they can offer smarter discounts based on data, protect their pricing power and avoid making mistakes that cut into their margins. This is a must in an era when pricing often overshadows other criteria in purchasing decisions, at the expense of value or brand loyalty.

Take the example of Goodyear, whose customers did not want to pay a premium for the benefit of an extended tread life. Realizing that positioning around its engineering complexity was not producing sales, Goodyear decided to instead price its tire models on the basis of how many miles they could be expected to last.[1]

Or say a company notices its customers spend more when they perceive a lower per-unit cost. The company might decide to offer tiered pricing levels rather than focusing on unit volume. If a business discovers that enterprise organizations spend more on hardware if the services are discounted, it might raise its hardware prices while offering discounted services to this customer segment. Perhaps a company realizes excellent renewal rates. It might reduce the price of the first-year subscription to attract more new customers. This type of strategic, dynamic pricing is only possible with a firm foundation of connected data and an integrated Quote-to-Cash process.

Complicating matters is the fact that today's global businesses typically employ a distributed workforce in remote offices, frequently change pricing and business rules, and realize a significant portion of revenues from timely renewals. That means anyone interacting with customers at any point in a deal needs accurate, nearly real-time information and decision-making capabilities at their fingertips. They can't be searching through disparate tools containing various pieces of information related to a customer to try to piece together an accurate view of the situation.

Yet with more and more layered channels emerging between businesses and their customers and the distribution channel getting more complex, deal status becomes more opaque. This is compounded by the need to accommodate sales through the indirect channel, which makes up a significant portion of revenue streams for many businesses. Additionally, the changing balance of power between businesses and their partners requires vendors to work out numerous other issues, such as:

---

[1]  Harvard Business Review, "How to Stop Customers from Fixating on Price," May 2010

- How to onboard and maintain mindshare with partners
- How and where partners can sell
- How to incentivize partners to sell their products and services (over alternatives or competitive offerings)
- How to pinpoint the right balance between product/service push and pull

Operating profitably in the face of all this complexity requires companies to package and sell their products differently from the way they have in the past, and traditional back-office systems are not designed to accommodate these needs.

## Staring down growing global competition and commoditization

As if that's not enough, global businesses are facing rising competition and threats of commoditization at every turn. A flattening world economy is permitting new innovations to appear abruptly from unexpected areas. Disruptive products and business models are often originating from outside of traditional markets with sudden speed, as consumers and corporations increasingly shop around worldwide. At the same time, product differentiation, intellectual property advantages and margins are increasingly vulnerable to the rapid emergence of alternatives.

Regardless of industry, the competitive climate has fundamentally changed: products are increasingly commoditized because of the following:

- Shifts to online sales (think bookstores getting undercut by Amazon)
- Lower barriers of entry (leading to faster appearance of new competitors)

- An expanded supply of a good or service, whether from domestic sources or from abroad

A 2014 study by Roland Berger Strategy Consultants (an international consultancy) found that 63% of all companies surveyed across 10 major industries are facing the commoditization of their products and services.[1]

It's no longer enough to sell a hard product: manufactured goods can always be sold for cheaper, and global competition drives down the margins fast. Instead, businesses are being forced to adopt a hybrid revenue model.

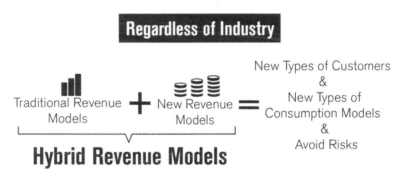

Consider activity trackers such as Fitbit. These devices provide value on their own—allowing the user to track various fitness activities, heart rate, and more. But increasingly, manufacturers of these devices are setting themselves apart by connecting to apps and wrapping subscription services around them. Perhaps someone who tracks their exercise activities using the Fitbit would qualify for a lower health insurance rate by downloading an app that feeds data to the insurance provider. Or perhaps the user would be eligible for a discounted gym membership, or sessions with a life coach. These types of value adds set the Fitbit apart from cheaper alternatives that lack these services.

That said, by adding these services, the manufacturer has also added complexity to its operations. It must track and share customer behavior via data coming through the device. It must also manage

---

[1]   Roland Berger Strategy Consultants, Escaping the Commodity Trap, April 2014

partnerships with those companies offering incentives for exercising. Imagine that Fitbit cuts a check to a life coach for every session with a Fitbit customer. The company needs to track upsell services used by the customer and manage and pay out against those.

The goal then is to escape the commodity trap—which is a situation where even complex products and services are downgraded to 'commodities,' with limited differentiation and where competition is primarily price-based.[1] To do so, Roland Berger advises global businesses to pull on the appropriate levers, ranging from ones with short-term impact to those with lasting impact. As shown in the table below, most of these levers are impacted by, or are managed within, the Quote-to-Cash process to significant degree. And that means to successfully enacting a strategy to avoid or climb out of a commodity trap, companies must establish a solid Quote-to-Cash foundation.

| | **Levers** | **Examples** |
|---|---|---|
| **Short-term levers** | 1 Apply marketing and sales actions | Advertising advanced pricing strategies, CRM, strategic product positioning |
| | 2 Upgrade bundle products with services for differentiation | Extend warranties ensure guaranteed availability, provide maintenance packages |
| **Med-term levers** | 3 Shift toward specific market segments | Specific products for developing countries, high-end customers, etc |
| | 4 Use innovation to differentiate products | Focus on R&D activities to gain/maintain technology leadership |
| | 5 Improve product and delivery quality | Guarantee limited failure rates/downtime, on-time in-full (OTIF) |
| | 6 Strengthen target cost/design-to-cost | Focus R&D activities on design-to-cost based on derived cost targets |
| **Long-term levers** | 7 Strategically align portfolio | Buy/Sell business units |
| | 8 Strategically align the business model | Introduce new revenue model, switch to higher step in value chain |
| | 9 Create a suitable organizational basis to react flexibly to strategic challenges | Set up small independent business units with P&L responsibility |

For instance, perhaps the threat is that competitors are producing their products and maintaining critical operations offshore to take advantage of cheaper labor. With proper insight into this issue, a company conducting the majority of its business in the U.S. could pinpoint the drawback of this approach. Namely that it is challenging to manage demand for smaller lots of products that need to be "personalized" to the needs of different customer segments, within shorter timeframes, unless the product is manufactured in the U.S. By positioning around this value proposition, the company could

---

[1] Ibid

command a higher price and still win business by offering product(s) that more closely match customers' specific needs with dramatically shorter lead times.

In addition, the company could boost the value of its offerings by analyzing the purchasing patterns of like customers in that sector to determine willingness to pay. Based on its findings, it could craft same-day maintenance and extended warranty service agreements that reinforce branding on quality (i.e., a premium brand). This would require tools to determine the optimal price and accurately forecast the business.

The ability to avoid the commodity trap requires that businesses can gain full and accurate visibility into every aspect and detail across their Quote-to-Cash process so they can make informed decisions about a strategic course of direction.

## Reacting to rising market volatility

The major trends we just walked through—the increasingly connected global economy, rising competition and commoditization, and rapid changes in buying preferences—are triggering abrupt shifts in supply and demand with greater frequency and intensity. And businesses need greater agility to operate in markets experiencing boom-and-bust phases.

We've seen repeated market volatility over the past fifteen years, with bubbles and market crashes experienced in such diverse sectors as high tech, communications, real estate, finance, automobile manufacturing, commodities and energy. These disruptions have impacted most major national economies, usually with benefits and challenges being distributed unevenly and at different times. Consider how several energy-producing countries benefited from high petroleum prices for a good number of years until the market suddenly declined precipitously.

Even in good times, a business should anticipate when and how downturns may suddenly unfold. A short-term perspective places the enterprise's survival at risk. Successfully projecting supply, demand, and buyer sentiments over a medium period of time ensures that the company can fully reap the rewards of its investments in products, capacity, sales, and marketing as circumstances allow.

An integrated Quote-to-Cash process allows companies to glean insights into market demand and pricing. This is made possible by mining the data flowing through quoting, contracting, ordering, billing and other processes. With a full view across all this data, companies can pinpoint patterns around what is selling, to whom (the key customer segments), at what price, at what rate (selling like hotcakes, slowing down), and so on.

Moreover, an integrated Quote-to-Cash process dramatically improves the crafting and selling of subscription-based products, executing renewals, and re-ordering across all channels. Handled well, these increase visibility into and predictability of revenue streams, enabling companies to respond quickly and effectively to market developments.

## Operating in a more highly regulated business climate

Many companies are facing the worst of all worlds: confronting markets undergoing radical transformation while at the same time having to comply with increasing regulation by governing bodies trying to maintain orderly markets. It's challenging enough to stay viable and relevant in the midst of ever-changing market dynamics. Add regulatory burdens to the mix and it's easy to see how a company can be crushed by the pressures.

At a minimum, just about every industry operates under some form of regulation when it comes to pricing and selling products (like antitrust measures, consumer protection laws, etc.). And all must be rigorous in following reporting standards for financial results. As a result, companies must be truthful about the cost of doing business: they must satisfy new accounting standards demanded of them by the Internal Revenue Service or other regulatory bodies, even when using creative discounting and rebating. This reality is further exacerbated in the face of emerging revenue models, such as aircraft engines or automobile tires with pricing based on consumption, and insurance premiums based on how the consumer's driving or exercise habits.

Let's assume a business is changing how it engages with customers: it must be explicit up-front about this, such as by outlining competitive risks in its annual report. And to report in this way, it needs a single source of truth about all deal-related details.

| COMPLEX PRODUCTS | GLOBAL COMPETITORS | MODERN BUYERS |
|---|---|---|
| ■ Products AND services<br>■ Software AND IoT packages<br>■ New, used and rentals | ■ Commoditization<br>■ Copycat manufacturing<br>■ Gray Markets | ■ E-Commerce and mobile<br>■ Mutiple sales channels<br>■ Social selling |
| Just selling equipment and not other complementary solutions results in | Not responding to changing business models will result in competitive switching | Channel conflict in e-commerce and partner commerce creates |
| **Smaller Deal Size** | **Lost Market Share** | **Missed Revenue** |

At the same time, companies in certain sectors are impacted by industry-specific regulations. Consider the Dodd-Frank Act, which requires all financial institutions with $50 billion in consolidated assets to submit annual reports (called "living wills"). These reports must address a variety of compliance items, including one specifically dealing with "critical vendors" that support the business. The financial institution must identify all vendors deemed critical to its core business. Then it must search through all contracts for those vendors to determine whether they contain required language related to continued operations in the event of financial distress. That represents a lot of work. Some banks have spent more than a year to complete this process.

Similar scenarios are playing out in other sectors, such as with "sunshine laws" in the U.S. for the life sciences industry. In France, the Conseil d'État mandated in 2015 that healthcare companies disclose the contractual remuneration paid to healthcare providers. Moreover, the court required manufacturers and marketers of cosmetics and tattoo products be held to the same standards as medical device and pharmaceutical firms. As increasing regulation spans different industries and crosses international borders, many companies find themselves taking on onerous tasks to comply.

## Companies across all industries faced with digital disruption

Think this does not apply to your company? Think again. Since 2000, "52% of the companies in the Fortune 500 have gone bankrupt, have been acquired, or have ceased to exist, due in large part to the disruption of traditional industry models by digital models."[1]

Consider John Deere, the manufacturing company that was founded in 1837. Recognizing that even farming is going digital, in 2012, the industry behemoth launched MyJohnDeere.com, a digital platform providing customers with real-time information about their farm operations, field locations and equipment performance. "This platform supports an ecosystem strategy that has allowed the company to establish new digital partnerships with bio-chemistry and agricultural hybridization leaders."[2]

By tapping into the data from 200,000 connected devices (in other words, tractors and other farm equipment) served by the platform, third parties are developing a range of applications, such as ones to

---

[1]  Constellation Research, Constellation's 2014 Outlook on Dominating Digital Business Disruption, February 10, 2014

[2]  Accenture Technology Vision 2015, Digital Business Era: Stretch Your Boundaries

track the weather and disposition of pesticides and fertilizers, soil conditions, and more. In this way, the platform serves as a marketplace connecting suppliers, dealers and farmers. In fact, John Deere's mission is to operate a marketplace—an App Store for agriculture, if you will—that generates hundreds of millions in revenue. By taking these steps, John Deere is staying relevant while satisfying the needs of the next-generation of customers.

Other businesses would be smart to pay heed. Research firm IDC predicts that "one-third of leaders in virtually every industry will be disrupted by competitors by 2018—newcomers and established—that leverage platforms to innovate new offerings, reach new customers, radically expand supply and go-to-market networks, and disrupt their industries' cost and profit models."[1]

And that only further complicates what it means to conduct business in today's world. Moreover, it further underscores the imperative to get the Quote-to-Cash process right. Not only do disjointed and manual Quote-to-Cash processes prevent enterprises from achieving the highest levels of performance, they actually result in negative consequences across the business. The table below displays a few of the ways that inferior Quote-to-Cash processes lead to enterprise-wide dysfunction.

It's no surprise that a manual, disjointed Quote-to-Cash process can ripple across the business to negative effect. Any issues that start "upstream" (for example, the wrong pricing or contracting terms) trickle down to operations and finance. But because the Quote-to-Cash process is so complex and cross functional, problems like this are often not discovered until someone in finance is reviewing the general ledger or balance sheet.

---

[1]  IDC, IDC Predictions 2015: Accelerating Innovation—and Growth—on the 3rd Platform, December 2014

| Finance | Sales | Marketing | Quoting Operations/ Order Management | Operations | Customer Service |
|---|---|---|---|---|---|
| Issues with tax, reporting and compliance due to a lack of consistent information | Relentless pressure to maintain or improve margins on all transactions | Missed opportunities due to the lack of competitive information | Lacks efficient system-driven compliance and validation checks, creating increased exposure to compliance risk | Sub-optimized fulfillment, production and logistics conditions due to poor order visibility | Poor service response and revenue leakage due to fragmented processes and limited visibility of data around service, contracts, warranties and entitlements |
| Revenue and profit forecasting challenges due to inadequate or conflicting data | Lost opportunities because many (if not most) deals require manual intervention | Inaccurate information leads to less competitive offers | Lack of seamless integration with quote, leading to data misalignment and erroneous order creation/ booking | Quoting channel partners hesitate to do business or even to maintain the partnership | Poor customer service due to limited visibility of data about customer installed base and its entitlements |
| Cannot generate timely, accurate invoices without intervening manually in the invoicing process after invoice creation | Incorrect or missing information leads to poor customer service and reducing effectiveness of cross-sell and upsell programs | Inaccurate information leads to overly generous offer and reduced profits | One-size-fits-all model for all business processes, including order review and management, leads to customer and channel partner dissatisfaction, prolonged order review and order booking cycle times | Supply chain visibility is minimal at best, making the fulfillment cycle and order status difficult or impossible to track | |
| | Manual price approvals slow deal velocity | | | | |

[1]

[1]  Source: PwC, Technology industry at the cross-roads: Transforming quote-to-cash operations, 2013

This messy process is clashing with a mandate tearing through companies across industries: the need to run faster while becoming easier to work with and streamlining customer interactions. Increasingly, this dictate is manifesting itself in a strategy that involves stabilizing and pulling data out of the back office (for example, from multiple ERP, financial, and fulfillment systems), and moving it into a new front office in the cloud. By shifting processes and systems from the traditional back office to a cloud-based front office, companies gain a common front end and modern interface to better processes and interactions. More specifically, they bring transparency to the back office/front office exchange of information, while their customers benefit from a better purchase experience.

Quote-to-Cash helps simplify the new layers defining today's business ecosystem—and more importantly, makes it possible to monetize the value. For example, assume a company sells through its own sales reps as well as partners and is dealing with a customer that starts the research process online. With ready access to the company's connected Quote-to-Cash processes, both the company's reps and the partners' agents would all refer to the same customer, product and service catalog detailing prices and discounting rules. As a result, the company's customers would see the same information as the direct and partner sales reps—and have the same interactions with the direct sales force and partner agents—for a true multi-channel experience.

### The value of seamless Quote-to-Cash

When businesses properly and adeptly manage the highly collaborative aspects of the Quote-to-Cash process, they provide visibility to everyone involved, and streamline sales and contracting, close a higher percentage of deals, boost customer satisfaction, and drive more revenues.

## Key takeaways

Driving profitable growth in today's business environment is anything but easy. As enterprises assess the host of challenges they face, it's wise to focus on areas and issues within their control, namely their internal processes and procedures. It's even smarter to focus on those with the most impact across the company, such as revenue, which brings us back to Quote-to-Cash. Optimizing this end-to-end process can yield tremendous rewards.

With an optimized Quote-to-Cash process, sales reps can see which product combinations are most profitable, which discounts, bundles and add-ons can increase a deal's value, and which deals are up for renewal. Legal can drive more favorable deals by flowing up-to-date Legal language from quotes to contracts, and Finance can recognize revenue faster and more accurately. Finally, when the Quote-to-Cash process is optimized, executives have the visibility to confidently assess cash flow, and ensure the business is running effectively.

### It's time to embrace a new way of doing business

"In the age of the customer, B2B buyers demand more transparency, convenience, and speed. As such, B2B buyers are forcing B2B sellers and their ecosystem partners (such as resellers, distributors, service providers, agents, and manufacturer sales reps) to rethink traditional selling models and harness technologies, both to deliver a superior customer experience and to drive agility and operational efficiency."

–Forrester, *Death of a (B2B) Salesman*
by Andy Hoar, April 13, 2015

# The Customer-Centered World
## Adapt or Die

In the last chapter we explored a world undergoing a confluence of changes forcing today's enterprises to operate in a more complex environment. But above all is the major trend of the world becoming increasingly customer-centric. Customers now expect companies to treat them as being central to all they do. These changes, create the need for more buying and selling channels, increase product complexity, pressure for more unique business and pricing models, induce more global competition and commoditization, and introduce more regulations. This new landscape puts immense pressure on organizations. If companies don't respond to these new realities they will be left behind. Organizations need to adapt to the changing market and business conditions by developing a sound strategy and taking methodical steps to spearhead change.

Though we aren't going to tackle the issue of change management, we are going to outline the critical elements that organizations must put in place to successfully adapt and win in today's business climate. And then we will explain why Quote-to-Cash is so important as an enabler for businesses to manage to the new realities of the modern, customer-centered world.

The most fundamental paradigm is that it is absolutely paramount that organizations become customer-centric. To deliver on this mantra and approach, organizations must:

- Be available to customers in every channel of their choice (i.e., be omni-channel)

31

- Interact and transact with customers as quickly—and accurately—as possible in the way customers want to interact and buy (i.e., virtually and via social and mobile channels)

And to enable all this, it turns out a strange phenomenon needs to happen. Business functions that were traditionally thought of as back-office functions like billing, revenue management and contracts now have to become front-office functions. Why? Because exposing this relevant data to customers means organizations can react faster to customer needs. This is a radical departure from the way most organizations think of their business processes today. The good news is that a modern architected Quote-to-Cash system can enable this in a way no other system can. Netting it out, organizations need to give customers direct access to information so the customer can engage with organizations in the way they choose.

Let's explore this in more depth.

## Embrace customer centricity

Today's world is a buyer's market. This fact alone is forcing companies to re-imagine how they interact with their customers. Even though there is so much talk across industries and B2B companies about the need to be customer-centric, many organizations fail to understand and define precisely what this means.

According to Gallup, "A customer-centric model is about more than focusing on the customer or having a defined customer experience; it is about putting the customer at the core of everything. The goal of this model is to make the customer organization more successful, both within its own business and within the context of its partnership with the company."[1] Unfortunately, through its research Gallup has found that, "From heavy manufacturing to pharmaceuticals to law firms, B2B companies across all industries are at risk of being

---

[1]  Gallup, Guide to Customer Centricity Analytics and Advice for B2B Leaders, 2016

replaced—not because of their products or prices, but because they are failing their customers."[1]

As Satya Nadella, CEO of Microsoft, says, "we need to continue to reach for the next level of customer centricity and obsession in everything we do—sales, marketing, services and product development. It's very important to have "one feedback loop" across all parts of the company with customer value and satisfaction at the center."

So how does a company determine whether or not it is truly customer-centric? A truly customer-centric business looks at everything from the customer's perspective. Ultimately, customers care most about how easy it is to do business with the company they are considering. But what does "easy to do business with" mean?

Many companies focus on the opportunity management part of the sales cycle largely because that is all Customer Relationship Management (CRM) systems can support. But that is only a very small part of what determines the overall customer experience with the company.

A customer is engaged with the company at numerous points before, during, and after purchasing a product or service. These interactions include when the salesperson is presenting the product or service, when the customer receives a quote, negotiates a contract, receives an invoice, accepts delivery of the product or service, receives the right rebate or promotion, and more. The company that is easy to do business with is the one that considers all customer touchpoints through the lens of the customer.

Again, Gallup research surfaced interesting findings around this. Gallup found that customers "scrutinize ease of doing business with the company" when evaluating vendor performance. According to the research-based consulting firm, "ease of doing business" equates to a few factors, including "the simplicity and transparency of the company's processes."[2]

---

[1]  Ibid

[2]  Ibid

So how does this come into play around the Quote-to-Cash process? Consider just the critical, legally binding contract management element of the Quote-to-Cash process. More than 80% of business commerce transactions are tied to a contract—and these critical documents determine the trading relationship with your organization. They spell out who is paying the company, what amount they are paying, how long they'll be paying, their obligations to deliver… essentially, contracts are the blueprint of your trading relationship with each customer.

Armed with insight into contract data, a company's Legal team can be empowered to make better business decisions, and simplify operations across Finance, Sales, Marketing and executive teams. And when these teams are armed with right contract information, they can ensure significantly better interactions with the customer.

Contrast this with an inefficient, opaque contract management process that noticeably, directly and negatively impacts customer relationships, Days Sales Outstanding (DSOs), top- and bottom-line revenue and company liability. In fact, in an Apttus survey of legal and contracting professionals who agree they lack automated contract management, 61% admitted they're not easy to do business with and 60% stated they're not viewed as being responsive.

These are alarming statistics. In a customer-driven world, speed, convenience and efficiency mean everything.

## Serving customers across channels

As described above, being customer-centric is about delivering world-class experiences anywhere a customer is interacting with the company, not just during a salesperson's engagement with the customer. To answer buyers' demands for easy, rapid access to products and services through their channel of choice, today's organizations cannot afford to prioritize any single channel. Instead, organizations must enable and support a multi-channel strategy for any touch point with the customer. In essence, the goal is to become channel neutral, making it possible for customers to traverse whichever channel—or channels—they choose as they go through the process of buying, ordering and using a product or service. These channels should include direct selling, self-service, social, mobile, the Internet of Things, augmented reality and any other potential touchpoints with a human.

> Research by McKinsey & Company shows that, on average, "a B2B customer will regularly use six different interaction channels throughout the decision journey..."[1]
>
> [1]  McKinsey Quarterly, Do you really understand how your business customers buy?, February 2015

Thinking about that in the context of being customer-centric, omni-channel or multi-channel selling is a way to dramatically improve the ease of doing business for customers in a way that makes financial sense for a company. While companies have been selling through multiple channels for years, a fresh look at omni-channel processes can immediately yield happier customers, sustainable competitive advantage and profitable growth. This is because a more touchless model, providing as much information as possible, empowers the customer and makes them more likely to buy.

While, by definition, omni-channel encapsulates all channels, emphasis should be given to the digital realm. As we are seeing, the rise of the digital channel is being felt across industries. Gartner states that, "In the 2015 Gartner CEO survey, respondents said that 41% of overall revenue would be attributable to digital by 2019. In 2016, this figure grew to 46%."[1]

In fact, Forrester found that 93% of B2B buyers say they prefer to buy online once they've decided what to buy and just need to make the purchase.[2] We can thank Amazon for that. When we know what we want, we want to buy it quickly and easily—whether we're making a purchase in our personal lives or in our professional lives. How do we

[1]  Gartner "Digital Commerce Hype Cycle 2016" 7 July 2016
[2]  Forrester, *Death of a (B2B) Salesman,* April 14, 2015

find what we want? By being empowered with the right information provided by the seller utilizing any channel including search, social media and others.

Moreover, McKinsey & Company has found that "Empowered [B2B] purchasers increasingly demand real-time digital interactions supported by tools such as product configurators and price calculators."[1]

Despite all of this, just 25% of B2B companies today actively sell online, which means B2B companies are drastically behind the curve and losing opportunities to delight their customers. From the company perspective, this translates into lost revenues. Here's why, according to Forrester Consulting:

- Approximately 80% of B2B firms selling directly to customers online said their omni-channel customers are "profitable."[2]

- 72% [of B2B companies] agreed that omni-channel customers are worth substantially more to them than a single-channel customer, and 51% said these customers have a higher lifetime value."[3]

- Online B2B customers are more active than offline customers and have higher average order volumes.[4]

- 75% of B2B buyers would buy again from the same supplier because of that supplier's omni-channel capabilities."[5]

The goal of an omni-channel strategy is to provide customers with a smooth experience, regardless of which channel they started with and in which one they end. While many companies have already sold through multiple channels for decades, few have been able to coordinate omni-channel efforts to maximize the customer experience

---

[1]  McKinsey Quarterly, Do you really understand how your business customers buy?, February 2015

[2]  Forrester Consulting, Building The B2B OmniChannel Commerce Platform Of The Future, November 2014

[3]  Ibid

[4]  Forrester Consulting, Online And Mobile Are Transforming B2B Commerce, October 2013

[5]  Ibid

as well as company profits. The challenge companies face is how to make all these different points of interaction a high-quality, unified experience where the brand, products and pricing are consistent.

In my travels I have come across many unbelievable stories about the impact of this disconnected multi-channel selling. One was from a very large multi-billion dollar organization that sells its products online and via telesales people. This company relied on huge systems, but the systems were not integrated. Many times when a customer calls the telesales person, the first question the rep asks is, "Did you visit our website to configure the product you want?" Now you would think the rep wants to find this out in order to understand whether or not it's necessary to configure the product for the customer. But in fact it's because the pricing the rep gives to the customer is quite different to the pricing that appears on the web because they are using a different system—and the systems are not integrated. So the rep asks the customer to walk them through the exact configuration they did on the website, click-by-click. As the customer is telling the rep, the rep is following the steps so they can quote competitively to the pricing the customer saw on the website—a scenario that is staggering in today's modern world.

## Conduct business at tomorrow's fast pace

Hand in hand with the growing customer demand to conduct business across multiple channels is the expectation for fast, frictionless interactions and transactions. This trend will accelerate and require most companies to retool their processes and systems. After all, other than startups and "born-digital" companies, most businesses have built their systems and processes with products, supply chains and channels—rather than customers—in mind. To complicate matters—as we explored in the previous chapter—these systems and processes are more often than not, disconnected and siloed.

Not only does this mean a companies' systems and processes fail to support the corporate goal of satisfying customers' expectations in the omni-channel world, they also inhibit the speed and agility that customers demand. According to Gallup, "Customers want the companies they do business with to work faster and with more flexibility."[1] Companies that can expose more and more information to self-empower the customer relieve themselves of many tasks and yet end up with a happier customer.

Compounding this is the impact of social media. Companies that fail to satisfy customer expectations for higher service levels, support and satisfaction stand to suffer greatly at the hands of customers who share their displeasure with their extended business networks online.

And though a customer-centric approach is imperative in today's business world, companies must still look at their current business processes in order to understand what is needed to become customer-centric. Are you designed for your customers or are you designed for your company?

From an IT perspective, utilizing disparate applications—even if they have been integrated—is both potentially insecure and definitely complex and costly. For example, each of the different systems require IT parameters that include:

- Integrating data flow
- Managing disparate security policies
- Managing upgrades and compatibilities to other systems
- Deciding on systems of record
- Enabling multiple support channels
- Interacting with and managing multiple vendors

Even when companies spend considerable time and money to successfully integrate specific, siloed processes, end users (for example, sales reps, finance, and legal) still face challenges in the form of:

- Learning new applications

---

[1]  Gallup, Guide to Customer Centricity Analytics and Advice for B2B Leaders, 2016

- Getting comfortable with new user interfaces
- Navigating disparate workflows and approval systems
- Managing data synchronization issues

When it comes to the Quote-to-Cash process, other key problems in this siloed approach include:

- Entering the same manual data into multiple systems
- Managing complex approvals across multiple systems
- Tracking audit trails
- Handling manual dropouts
- Responding to changes in business requirements
- Reporting on accurate and real-time data
- Ensuring enterprise controls
- Observing corporate governance

Compounding matters is the need to manage the mass of documents created throughout the Quote-to-Cash process: quotes, price budgets, contracts, sales orders, and so on.

Nothing in the traditional, siloed approach—such as relying on slow, ERP-centric infrastructure—supports the need for speed in today's business world. And that's precisely why so many companies are moving critical, integrated Quote-to-Cash processes to the cloud. The cloud enables companies to transcend the confines of onsite IT, complex and disparate systems, and manual processes. In doing so, the cloud is helping companies revolutionize the way their business processes are managed. In fact, the cloud empowers organizations to deploy and scale entirely new business models and revenue streams extremely rapidly without IT complexity. But perhaps most importantly, these cloud applications make it possible to make rapid changes, easily expose data and quickly give customers what they want and need.

> Hiding behind slow, ERP-centric infrastructure is now a tired excuse because more and companies are finding born-in-the-cloud solutions to be a competitive advantage. Cloud-based solutions are easier to deploy, result in lower total cost of ownership, encourage broader and faster user adoption, and offer greater flexibility and superior capabilities along with a dramatically faster roadmap.

## Creating a new front office

As businesses recognize the need to operate with more speed and scale beyond the traditional boundaries of their business and the systems and process that support it, a growing number of them are creating a "new front office." They are starting to move what were largely thought of as back-office functions—and often disjointed solutions powered by ERP—to the cloud powered by front-office systems. This enables customer-facing interactions to be almost real time. In other words, companies are creating cloud-based front offices that look radically different from today's front offices. This new front office essentially "moves" the systems typically thought of as belonging in the back office, to the front office to enable a true customer-centric experience on the front end. And because these systems live in the cloud, this front office makes it possible for companies to improve customer relationships, become easier to work with, and scale faster than ever before.

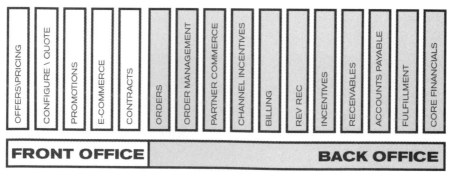

*Traditional Front and Back Office*

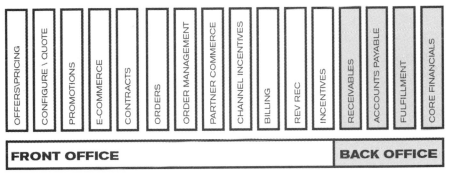

*New Front and Back Office*

## The Uber example

Uber as a company and business model is a spectacular example of the changing front office. Uber entered the market with a radically disruptive business model, initially focused on making the taxi industry more efficient. The seemingly simple business model ended up being one so disruptive that the entire world reacted to it. In fact, in many parts of the world, Uber has been banned for the fear of massive disruption to traditional protected industries.

That aside, the genius of Uber's business model is a perfect example of how customers access data traditionally thought of as "back office" and get a substantially better experience because of it.

Let's start with the product. When standing on the side of the road waiting for a traditional taxi, you have no idea about the "product"— the quality of the actual car, the track record of the driver, etc. In other words, the customer has no visibility into the "product data." With Uber, one click on the mobile device tells the customer the car and driver details, ratings by previous customers, rate options, and more. You get complete visibility into the product before even seeing it, allowing you to choose whether or not to accept the car and driver (the "product"). Product data in most industries is included in PLM (Product Lifecycle Management) systems which are large back-office applications.

Now let's talk about the supply chain and delivery. You might wait for a traditional taxi on the side of a road for either a short time or a very long time depending on taxi density and availability in your area. You don't know when your product is going to arrive. The supply chain delivering your product is opaque. You have no visibility into availability. However, Uber's mobile application lets you know exactly where all available cars are, how much time it will take the car to reach you and, once in the car, how long it will take to arrive at your destination. This is all back-office information now available directly to the customer.

Then there is billing. When getting into a traditional taxi, you don't know how much the ride will end up costing. With Uber, you know how much you'll pay before you even get into the car. Again, back-office information available to the customer.

Each of these processes are historically deemed to be "back-office" functions in most companies. But by exposing them to the "front office" and letting customers see the data, the customer can make better decisions and have a substantially better experience. Uber's market cap is tens of billions of dollars because of its customer-centric model.

The cloud impact on customer experiences

Migrating to unify IT systems and processes around the customer experience, companies are finding the cloud makes it easier to move from a disjointed state to an integrated one. This aligns perfectly with the Aberdeen Group's view that "The omni-channel world we live in requires online, cloud-ready orchestration of events and activities across an increasingly multi-party end-to-end supply chain."[1] By making this shift, companies can more adeptly orchestrate all the elements that go into serving their customers better than anyone else—and they can do it at a pace that will satisfy customer expectations.

It's no wonder IDC poses that 'Cloud First' will become the new mantra for—and the cloud will serve as the new core of—enterprise IT.

[1]  Aberdeen Group, Profitable Supply Chain Execution with Customer- and Event-Driven Optimization, January 2016

In fact, IDC suggests that to succeed going forward, companies will need to call upon technologies including cloud to "create competitive advantage through new offerings, new business models, and new customer, supplier, and distributor relationships."[1]

And there's no time to waste. Many companies are already harnessing the power of the cloud and realizing amazing results. According to the Aberdeen Group, "From the customer or demand-group of processes, the cloud-based leaders are better connected across processes from order to deliver/service/cash."[2]

## Summary: Forging a new path forward

Companies responding to the call for customer-centricity cannot afford to try to manage business in a siloed fashion. In fact, it's dangerous to do so, putting the organization at risk of missed opportunities and even costly oversights and mistakes that could undermine operations all together.

Rather, they must heed the mandate to embrace a new approach, one that recognizes the need to support omni-channel business and move at faster speeds than ever before. At the center of it all is the end-to-end Quote-to-Cash process. By moving this process out of disjointed systems and into a Quote-to-Cash system, companies across industries are creating a new front office that helps them revolutionize the way they go to market, empower their customers, and gain advantages because of it.

---

[1] Forbes, Transform Or Die: IDC's Top Technology Predictions For 2016, November 10, 2015

[2] Aberdeen Group, Profitable Supply Chain Execution with Customer- and Event-Driven Optimization, January 2016

# 3 Quote-to-Cash
## The Most Critical of all Business Processes

**M**aking major changes so that your company becomes easier to do business with requires a well-considered process that is agile and customer responsive. Because the Quote-to-Cash process connects the front-office CRM system to the back-office ERP system, it becomes the single most important business process that drives revenue and profitability. Even more, it becomes the underpinning function to making your company "easier to do business with."

Quote-to-Cash is at the epicenter of every company's revenue process and has become the key to making customers successful. Arguably it is the most important process for businesses to master today, covering everything from configuring products and services, pricing, quoting, negotiating and executing contracts, fulfilling orders, invoicing, billing, managing and recognizing revenue, handling renewals and much more.

The fundamentals of the Quote-to-Cash business process have been around for a long time. Companies provide quotes during the pre-sales phase, regardless of the customer's chosen channel. Then they create a contract during the sales phase, and must finally account for revenues. But the way companies perform these functions is beginning to change and will further change radically as organizations start adjusting to how customers want to engage and conduct business. The key is to optimize the process in order to sell in the modern world.

Let's define Quote-to-Cash in the following ten key steps:

## The 10 Key Steps in Quote-to-Cash

Quote-to-Cash begins when during the opportunity management part of the sales cycle the customer expresses an early interest to buy and asks for indicative pricing or a quote. The customer could be buying directly from a salesperson or through a channel like a website or mobile device. Regardless, this first interaction kicks off a series of follow-on steps that constitute Quote-to-Cash.

### Step 1: Product Selection and Configuration

In this step, an ideal combination of products and services is assembled or configured to satisfy the customer's requirements. First a salesperson must identify the right combination of goods and services to recommend to the customer. Depending on the complexity of the company's product lines, this can be more difficult than one would think. For example, if the products come with a variety of options, sub options, upgrades and services—such as warranties or rebates—product service configuration can present multiple opportunities for error.

To successfully navigate product configuration, skilled reps must listen to the customer to surface their needs, and then recommend a combination of products and services that best align with this. While the best reps can do this more naturally, it gets tricky when they are dealing with a constantly changing product catalog, thousands of SKUs, high sales rep turnover, or rapid growth. To enable *all* reps to be configuration experts, organizations need an automatic way to guide reps to the right product. If a customer is buying through an indirect channel, the same is needed to enable the customer to rapidly select and configure the chosen product or service.

### Step 2: Pricing

At this stage, a salesperson generates a price, usually based on a list. Then, if allowed, discounts, promotions or bundles are applied to the initial quote. Identifying the right price is critical because at this point, the entire revenue of your company is essentially being determined.

Pricing can be an incredibly complicated function. There are whole classes—and even degree programs—dedicated to defining an effective pricing strategy. However, in the Quote-to-Cash world, "pricing" refers to the set of rules that dictate how Sales can come up with a price, and what creative incentives they can offer the customer to ensure the right outcomes.

Pricing is the best way to influence behavior—not only a customers' behavior but the behavior of reps and partners too. For that reason, it should be determined strategically. In an ideal world, pricing should:

- Give sales reps the ability to push deals across the finish line without impacting deal profitability
- Be flexible enough to change with the market
- Be competitive but allow for differentiation

## Step 3: Quoting

After pricing, a quote is generated, approved and sent to the customer. Quotes are an extremely important part of the sales cycle. Not only are they the blueprint for the sales contract, the quotes are often the first impression a company makes on a potential customer. Quotes provide an opportunity to make a strong brand impression and demonstrate excellence to the customer. But quotes can also introduce risk. While an accurate, polished quote is a step toward closing, a delayed, error-filled quote can leave a bad taste in the prospective customer's mouth, leading that person to question how your company operates.

Quoting can cause a lot of stress during the sales process too. Effective quoting requires both speed and accuracy, which can be hard to balance depending on your systems, processes and corporate culture. Everyone wants the first-mover advantage, but quality control is equally important. To be successful, companies need a quote approval process that introduces control but not bottlenecks. When too many people need to weigh in on the quote, or too many people across different buildings, geographies and time zones need to approve, it's a set-up for trouble. On the other hand, without a proper review process, quotes will likely include mistakes and may not represent the right revenue opportunity for your company.

### Step 4: Contract Creation

Once the quote has been reviewed with the customer and the customer wants to buy from the company, a contract or order form is created. Whether called "orders" or "contracts," all deals end with an agreement that includes a set of terms, conditions and, of course, the agreed-upon pricing. Business agreements can carry a lot of risk, and effective contract management is the best way to prevent that risk from impacting the revenue stream. When it comes to protecting a business, details matter—especially when significant revenue is at stake.

As contracts are created, it's important to ensure that the right people have visibility and input into anything that could introduce risk to the deal. Examples of potential risk vary depending on industry, product and service but examples include built-in renewal clauses, ramp pricing, termination clauses, opt outs and more. If an enterprise wants to give multiple people in the organization the ability to create contracts, it's best to rely on an internal, self-service tool, where contracts can be requested—and the correct language populated—automatically.

### Step 5: Contract Negotiation

At this stage, contract terms and clauses are negotiated, with each party redlining the documents. Anyone who has been involved in contract negotiation knows that these living, changing documents always represent a compromise. That's why it's important to start negotiating from a position of strength. Organizations can set themselves up for success here by paying close attention to the terms and conditions, and employing a thorough review process before the contract ever reaches the customer.

Once negotiations are under way, it's critical to get detailed visibility into what is changing in the contract. It's equally important to give Legal the ability to quickly intercede if something is added or removed that will negatively impact the financial aspects of the deal. That said, businesses don't want their expensive Legal resources combing through contracts line-by-line. Instead, these resources are best applied to manage exceptions. That means the ability to quickly identify changes or irregularities and then managing them to the best outcome for both parties is important.

And if a company is negotiating a deal on its trading partner's paper, getting visibility into how the third party's terms and conditions differ from the company's own standard language is essential for effective due diligence. Plus, it will enable the effective negotiation of the contract.

### Step 6: Contract Execution

Now an approved contract is signed and the deal is finalized. Getting the contract inked is the last thing anyone wants slowing down deals. That's why it's important to make it as easy as possible for customers to return signed agreements. To avoid making clients waste any time printing out a document, walking it around the office for signatures, and potentially forgetting about it, e-signature tools can provide a faster, more automated way to close deals. E-signature tools give visibility into who has already signed the document and where the bottlenecks might be. They also make it easy to send laggards a gentle reminder to keep the process moving along.

### Step 7: Order Fulfillment

Next the order is received, processed and delivered. Once a contract is signed, Operations (usually a fulfillment center or a services implementation team) kicks into gear to ensure the right products are delivered to the customer rapidly. During this step, an integrated, streamlined process can give the visibility needed to stay abreast of in-flight changes to the order, as well as changing delivery conditions and requirements.

Ideally, the company should have ongoing visibility with the fulfillment center and support teams, so there are never surprises when a deal closes. To that end, it should also be able to flow order details from the quote to the contract and through to the enterprise resource management (ERP) system or order management system. Moreover, it should be able to easily feed these details into the CRM system to enable fast, more intelligent renewals.

### Step 8: Billing

At this stage, final charges are calculated and an invoice is sent to the customer. Billing can be complicated, but it's important to get it right, as it's an integral part of cash forecasting and revenue recognition. The billing schedule is what ultimately determines cash flow, so if the company isn't punctually billing customers or collecting the correct amounts, cash flow will suffer.

When invoices are incorrect, billing time frames are inflexible, or companies are slow to send the bill, they're telling their customers they don't care about making business easy. In other words, they're sending a bad signal to their customers. But when everything from pre-sales to sales is a smooth, streamlined process, billing is easy. For companies that can automatically pass everything captured in the quote to the contract and on to the finance team, getting correct terms, billing information, and renewal information is automatic. And that means the risk of frustrating customers dramatically decreases.

### Step 9: Revenue Recognition

At this point, cash is received from the customer and the question becomes how to recognize the revenue. Closing a deal and recognizing cash is not the same thing. Usually only those in Finance think about revenue recognition, but recognizing revenue incorrectly introduces a lot of risk. For public companies, revenue recognition is part of the valuation, and if poorly handled, can make the company's stock plummet!

Here's where it becomes critical that the important details in contract terms—like pricing, net payment terms and delivery schedules—are made available to the people producing the invoices. Flowing this information quickly and accurately "downstream," so to speak, makes it more likely that companies will recognize revenue correctly, and keep cash flowing smoothly.

### Step 10: Renew

In today's world, it's just as vital to manage customer retention and drive recurring revenue. For many businesses, an enormous percentage of revenue comes from repeat or subscription customers, so the ten steps outlined here become an ongoing process. Even if the company isn't selling a service or a subscription, there is still tremendous revenue potential in the customer base from upsells and cross-sells. And that's why it's important to stay on top of contract renewals and customer buying history. It's also why so many best-in-class organizations have adopted Quote-to-Cash solutions to shorten renewal cycle times, increase renewal deal size and reduce churn.

The Quote-to-Cash process impacts almost everyone and every process in an organization.

Let's examine how Quote-to-Cash affects the following key departments in a company—Sales, Marketing, Finance, Legal, Operations, and IT—and some of the key challenges these departments face in the quest for cash. In each case, we highlight the department's main responsibilities and concerns when it comes to handling their portion of the Quote-to-Cash process the best way possible.

| SALES / SALES OPERATIONS | FINANCE | LEGAL | OPERATIONS | MARKETING | IT |
|---|---|---|---|---|---|
| Proposal Pricing Quoting Negotiation | Billing Revenue Forecast | Contracts | Order Invoice Customer Service Renewals | Promotions Pricing Channels | Process Maintenance Scale |

## Sales and Sales Operations

Here's what Sales and Sales Operations think about in the context of Quote-to-Cash.

"If I can wrap upsells and cross-sells and offer intelligent discounts and bundling options, I know I can increase the size of the deal. But most importantly, the quote has to be accurate, and I have to get it to the customer fast."

Sales and Sales Operations professionals are usually *very* familiar with the challenges of the Quote-to-Cash process—especially if that process is manual. When sales cycles drag on or reps can't meet their quotas, it's a sure sign that the Quote-to-Cash process needs an overhaul.

What makes the Quote-to-Cash process difficult for Sales? Common challenges include a changing or growing product catalog, disagreements around what discounts to offer, and difficulties or delays getting quotes and contracts approved.

## Sure Signs Quote-to-Cash is a Problem for Sales

- Reps respond slower than competitors to customer requests
- Execs are needed to approve even routine deals
- Reps lack the product and catalog knowledge to make effective customer recommendations
- Reps get bogged down in manual, error-prone processes
- Reps are unable to create bundles and kits for solution selling
- Low quota attainment and high sales turnover
- Inability to upsell and cross-sell
- Low customer renewal rates
- Renewals are not given priority as revenue opportunities

- Rogue discounting is common and tolerated
- Sales quotes on products that can't be delivered
- Quotes are unprofessionally presented, poorly branded
- Inability to respond to competitive pricing pressures

## Marketing

Here's what's top of mind for Marketing when it comes to Quote-to-Cash. "We are feeling more and more pressure to contribute to revenues, which means pushing through new sales while generating more sales from existing customers—both through direct sales and the channel. But it's challenging to ensure we're delivering the best results possible without visibility into the entire customer experience and transparency throughout our partner ecosystem."

Marketing may seem like a department that is outside the deal flow, but nothing could be further from the truth. In many organizations today, Marketing is increasingly being charged with driving revenues and proving their impact. To that end, they must partner with third parties to develop and promote value-added services and solutions, which involves orchestrating promotions, pricing, and experiences across channels. They must also determine which promotions are working, and ensure the product and service positioning, packaging, and pricing they've defined are observed during the sales process. Equally important, Marketing needs to cultivate customer loyalty, and continually identify opportunities to better serve the market going forward.

To succeed, Marketing needs full visibility into customer choices and experiences during the deal and beyond, as well as any partner actions that affect the customer. A connected Quote-to-Cash process provides Marketing with this information along with access to data the team can analyze to determine the impact of their programs and initiatives.

## Sure Signs Quote-to-Cash is a Problem for Marketing

- Limited visibility into buying trends, market conditions and customer preferences
- Declining customer mindshare
- Difficulty segmenting markets/customers with confidence
- Difficulty in bundling products, or making changes to product bundles
- Unclear product positioning and product value
- Too many price lists and outdated or contradictory pricing
- Misaligned pricing with market demand
- Inability to change pricing easily or quickly
- Slow to launch promotions and/or limited demand generated by promotions
- High shopping cart abandonment rates

### Finance

Finance has its own set of concerns when it comes to Quote-to-Cash. "Our shareholders expect us to provide accurate revenue forecasts. But it's a moving target. Invoice credits, performance bonuses, special discounts, non-standard payment terms, product bundles, regional differences—they're all over the place and drastically impact when we're allowed to realize revenue."

When considering who is involved in an optimized deal flow, Finance may not be the first department that comes to mind. But Finance is chiefly concerned with revenue growth and profitability. Not to mention, today's CFOs are under a lot of pressure to drive effective operations, and achieve better business results in new, innovative ways.

For Finance to succeed, the financial process must be efficient and transparent—visibility is the key. An effective Quote-to-Cash process is incredibly helpful to Finance because the same data that is found in contracts—like pricing, renewal uplifts, and expirations—can be used to more accurately forecast revenue. And when this data connects with back end systems, it can be used to assess deal profitability.

## How to Tell When Quote-to-Cash is a Problem for Finance

- Limited visibility into spending across various lines of business
- Lack of insight into customer obligations and increase clauses
- Revenue is left on the table
- Contracts can't be found
- Rogue discounting and reps turning unprofitable deals to hit numbers
- Billing schedules frequently do not align with contract terms
- Manual effort needed to map rogue deal structures to approved financial policies
- Inefficiencies to collect revenue after the deal is closed
- Difficult to track or collect on complex invoices for swaps, upgrades, co-terminations and true-ups
- Contracts are paid above agreed-upon rates
- Takes too long to monetize acquired products through current channels
- Legacy sales systems are expensive to upgrade/update

## Legal

Here's what's often top of mind for Legal around the Quote-to-Cash process: "It's always a back-and-forth struggle between wanting to help Sales close deals quickly and making sure they include the necessary terms—and the most up-to-date language—to avoid putting our company at risk."

Legal's primary responsibility is to ensure legal compliance, and manage corporate risk. Time is often divided between putting out fires (i.e. "We need this contract immediately!") and ensuring the business is taking the proper steps to avoid risk. Legal's biggest challenge is often visibility: if Legal can't see it, they can't control it. While Legal's preference is to be meticulous and examine contracts with a fine-tooth comb, the team is also pressured by Sales to get out of the way so deals can be closed fast.

For manual, paper-based Legal departments, ensuring compliance is a challenge! Without legal playbooks or templates, every contract is a one-off proposition, contract cycles lag, and errors increase.

## When Quote-to-Cash is a Problem for Legal

- No visibility into contract changes, operational challenges and bottlenecks
- Inconsistent approval process for contracts
- No visibility into expiring contracts, renewals and compliance
- Outdated and inconsistent legal language and errors in agreements
- Unfavorable vendor contracts automatically renew without review
- Non-standard legal language and errors in agreements
- No visibility into contract compliance, changes or amendments
- Unanticipated fines and litigation costs

## Operations

Operations has yet another perspective on the Quote-to-Cash process. "We carry the company on our back, and we do it with fragmented processes, and with limited visibility into customer data, service contracts, warranties and entitlements."

By "Operations," we are referring to a wide range of roles and responsibilities, which can even include professional services groups, call centers, or customer success teams, alongside the more traditional inventory and logistics groups. For most operations teams, efficiency and costs are a top concern. When there is no integration between quotes, contracts, and order fulfillment, order errors, expensive rework costs, and supply chain inefficiencies cause immense headache and grief.

## How You Know Quote-to-Cash is a Problem for Operations

- Limited visibility into transactions in flight and how they impact business strategy
- It takes too long to collect revenue after the deal is closed
- No visibility into operational challenges and bottlenecks
- High operational and rework costs
- Legacy sales systems are expensive to upgrade/update
- Rogue supplier spend goes unchecked and unnoticed
- Inability to handle payments for credit cards, ACH transactions and purchase orders
- Bundles and kits are often delivered with missing parts
- Disconnected systems and manual processes

## IT

IT's concern about the Quote-to-Cash process is how to best support all the elements across departments that contribute to the Quote-to-Cash process. "We're responsible for making fragmented processes work across the company, and enabling enterprise-wide visibility into all the data that goes into these processes."

At the highest levels, most IT teams are charged with driving rapid business innovation, making the business more agile, and ensuring technology can scale with growth. This ties in closely with the following top-of-mind issues: system deployment, maintenance, and upgrades, costs, enabling the latest technologies, and maintaining secure operations.

## Signs that Quote-to-Cash Causes IT Problems

- Disconnected systems and manual processes
- Limited connections between data housed in disjointed systems
- Spreadsheets, spreadsheets, spreadsheets
- Legacy systems are expensive to upgrade/update
- More budget spent on system maintenance than on system innovation
- Users not using all the tools available to them

## Why a Holistic Quote-to-Cash Process Matters

As we've outlined in this chapter, the Quote-to-Cash process involves many functions and impacts numerous departments across the company. While many organizations often treat the various stages in the Quote-to-Cash process as separate steps, it's critical to view and enable these in a holistic manner. Only in this way can businesses handle this process as adeptly and accurately as possible while enabling the utmost enterprise-wide visibility and efficiencies.

As the single link between top-line growth, bottom-line results and customer satisfaction, Quote-to-Cash relies on the collective intelligence of the enterprise. Accurate quotes, proposals, contracts and orders rely on the smooth flow of all data and processes within an enterprise. Businesses that achieve this level of connectedness create value for themselves and their partners and customers. Simply put, streamlining and automating Quote-to-Cash helps companies move revenue while reducing risk, boosting company-wide efficiency and increasing customer satisfaction.

# 4

# Intelligent Quote-to-Cash
## The Outcomes-Focused Era

In the previous chapters, we defined the key elements of the Quote-to-Cash process and explored each of these elements in depth. We have shown how critical these processes are to a customer-centric business approach and the need for agility to be competitive in today's market. Automation of the Quote-to-Cash process can become a key element in achieving these business objectives. But after having been involved in hundreds of customer engagements, we have observed several very interesting phenomena. The most important observation of which is that automating the process itself doesn't necessarily provide you the business outcome you may be looking for.

The goal of the vast majority of enterprise applications is to automate a manual process. This is typically accomplished through the implementation of a system that incorporates functionality for employees to do their jobs along with workflow rules guiding them to execute the right process. For instance, the reason you put a quoting tool in place is to make sure your employees are following the rules: quoting the right products with the right options, pricing them properly and getting the right approvals. The reasons are similar for a contract management tool: selecting the right initial contract template, using the right fallback provisions when a contract is negotiated, storing the documents in a simple, easy-to-use and accessible repository, and more. And for billing tools your goal is to manage your DSO (Days Sales Outstanding) while billing the right products and services, with the right payment terms, at the right time.

## How rules fall short

It's all about adhering to process rules, which is both necessary and important. The rules are either hard (you MUST take this action) or soft (I *recommend* you take this action). But either way, they are meant to successfully guide each customer engagement through the steps of the Quote-to-Cash process. In a nutshell, this is process automation.

Rules are useful when they help ensure the right activities are taking place at the right points in the process. Rules allow you to streamline operations and create an environment that reduces the number of exceptions users will encounter.

But from a business outcomes perspective, rules-driven systems don't necessarily give you the outcome you may seek. For starters, they operate on the (often false) premise that a process guru exists who knows what these rules should be and simply needs to configure the system accordingly.

Another critical limiting factor with rules is that they are 'static'. They represent the best thinking at a certain point in time based on retrospective information, which means they do not necessarily provide the best guidance for an unknown future. Meanwhile, your existing customers change their buying patterns over time, new competitors enter the market, existing ones offer new products and services, and you may launch new products in new geographies. With these new realities, old information is not just at risk of being rendered irrelevant. Perhaps the leading reason that businesses don't achieve their desired outcome with outdated Quote-to-Cash applications is their inability to identify trends and change rules at a rate that keeps pace with the market.

Finally, in practice, some process automation rules may end up automating and streamlining sub-optimal behavior. Even the simplest rules-based workflow engine not only highlights deficiencies but also may incent adverse outcomes.

Imagine a salesperson is working on a quote for a customer and submits pricing for an approval. What's interesting, as studies show, is that most of the time discount requests are approved without question. There are many reasons for this: the approver may not have any context, may not have enough information about what is being requested, and worst of all, doesn't want to be in the way of revenue opportunities for the company. Additionally, most people don't have the time or inclination to set up a meeting to discuss the issue with the parties involved, so they simply go ahead and approve it. After all, they approved the last 50 similar requests. They may certainly ask the questions, but getting in the way of revenue is frowned upon in most organizations. So it may be surprising to consider that a simple workflow engine may not affect the outcome to what you want—and in some cases may even cause additional delays!

And so what is important? The key is for the user to not only be able to manage their job and process, but to be motivated to change their behavior coupled with other information that gives them insights to do things better—so you actually achieve the business outcome desired. This requires the system to be not only process based applications, but behavior based applications and the use of machine learning or artificial intelligence capabilities. We call this *Intelligent* Quote-to-Cash. This is thinking and approach is revolutionary in the market and resulting in significant outcomes for corporations. Let's explore this more.

## Behavior-based Applications

Changing a user's behavior, making them perform the very best tasks for your company, is a key to achieving your desired business outcomes. This is accomplished, by understanding their motivators and aligning them to your organization's definition of success. We must understand what incentive motivates a particular user and then change that incentive at the exact point in the Quote-to-Cash process so the user changes behavior. That will result in a much higher likelihood of hitting a desired business outcome. The participants in the

Quote-to-Cash process vary from salespeople, sales support, finance, legal, operations and even C-level executives. Each of these players is motivated by a certain incentive model. If you can tap into these motivations and align them to the business outcome you seek, you can influence behaviors and increase the likelihood of hitting your desired business outcomes.

Let's continue with the sales example used above. Most salespeople are incented by money—sell more and therefore make more. So imagine: at the point of submitting the pricing approval for the quote, a compensation calculator is presented to that salesperson. It could show that the requested discount amount will lower their compensation. Because your company is trying to avoid a larger discount, the compensation incentive to the sales person will more than likely change their behavior specifically for salespeople who tend to be more liberal with high discounts. Conversely, by submitting pricing that doesn't require an approval because it's within the discount threshold you compensate the sales person a higher amount. Now the salesperson's behavior is more likely to result in a better outcome for your company than by them simply following a rule in a workflow engine.

Because you want to influence the behavior of individuals, you need the functionality in the tool to do that. You need behavior-based applications embedded in your Quote-to-Cash system because that's what dramatically increases the likelihood of improving your business outcome. But there are more than just behavior-based applications that can affect the outcome for your business.

## Machine Learning and Artificial Intelligence

Organizations today have access to an unbelievable amount of historical data. The age of "Big Data" is here. This data covers everything from past financial, operational and customer engagements, especially information about quotes, proposals and transactions. And while no shortage of effort has gone into creating descriptive charts and graphs that illustrate what *has* happened, very little has been done to apply these learnings in a prescriptive way to future customer engagements. In other words, little has been done to influence what *could* happen within the Quote-to-Cash process.

For example, if a company has a 1000-person direct sales team, the top 200 salespeople typically bring in a disproportionately large percentage of all new business. That's just the way sales works no matter how much we try to change it. But imagine if you were one of those 800 salespeople and while creating a quote, the system called upon organizational insights to present a new proposal. This proposal would resemble winning ones that were quoted by the top 200 salespeople for this type of customer situation. This deal is based on customers of similar profiles, but also incorporates certain upsells, cross sells and deal structures that the top 200 salespeople are typically able to execute.

## Organizations Procuring Enterprise Applications

Many organizations decide they want to buy a particular application because they have been led to believe it will solve a specific problem. But the vast majority of time, a single application genre itself will not help organizations achieve their desired business outcomes. Rather than start by buying an application, start by understanding the outcome you desire and then work backward to determine who within the organization needs what functional capability to drive toward that outcome. In other words, focus on the outcome, not the business application. Usually you will end up with a different set of applications than you would have originally selected.

Based on all this data, the system analyzes and presents an insight or "intelligence" to the salesperson—one that actually prescribes a better offering for the customer that is also better for your company. And in so doing the salesperson will also be better compensated. This can dramatically change the outcome of the customer engagement. And the same approach and technologies can be applied to many other use cases, ranging from discount management, cross selling, service management, the Internet of things and many more.

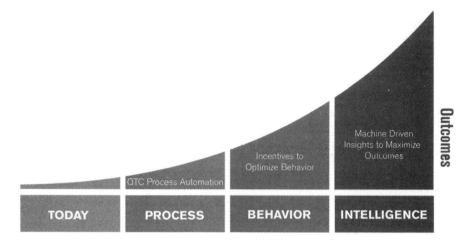

## Maximum impact and business outcome

This combination of process-based applications, behavioral applications and artificial intelligence applications provide an unbelievably powerful combination that will dramatically change the outcome of your organization. If you want to maximize the benefit of a Quote-to-Cash system, you must incorporate these three categories of applications. In doing so, you will be delivering on your revenue goals in a far superior way compared to your competition. This is *Intelligent Quote-to-Cash*.

# 5 Quote-to-Cash in the Multi-Channel World

**M**ost businesses find themselves supporting both direct channels (selling directly to customers or having them come to your website, E-Commerce and mobile options) and indirect channels (including distributors, agents, OEMs, brokers, dealers, agents, resellers, etc). Every channel plays a strategic role in the customer experience and it's imperative for companies to enable a modern multi-channel approach in order to provide a good customer experience and to gain a single view of customers' engagement with your company. But how does Quote-to-Cash come into play in a multi-channel business?

First let's define "multi-channel" versus "omni-channel." Multi-channel selling refers to companies leveraging a mix of B2B direct and partner activities in support of sales across different channels (with direct sales in the field, through a dealer, or on a website). Omni-channel commerce refers to companies orchestrating marketing and sales functions across multiple touchpoints to deliver seamless buying experiences to prospects and customers.

Given the availability of the internet and simplicity of technology access, it's no surprise that business purchases are increasingly moving to digital channels. According to industry analysts firms Gartner and Forrester Research, B2B E-Commerce in the United States alone is close to $1 trillion in annual transaction value.[1] No wonder Amazon launched Amazon Business, a marketplace on Amazon.com tailored to business buyers. According to Prentis Wilson, the Vice President of Amazon Business, "Amazon Business delivers a new and expanded

---

[1] Internet Retailer, 2015 Guide to B2B E-Commerce

marketplace that brings the selection, convenience and value of Amazon to business customers, manufacturers and sellers with the additional selection, features and back-end integration businesses need to save time and money."[1]

At their core, digitally enabled channels make the customer engagement process easy, whether they are a repeat customer or making their first purchase. And a smoother buying process translates into a company that customers enjoy doing business with—a critical factor that we discussed in chapter two.

## Drivers for channel shift

"What is your chief reason for shifting more work purchases online from offline?"

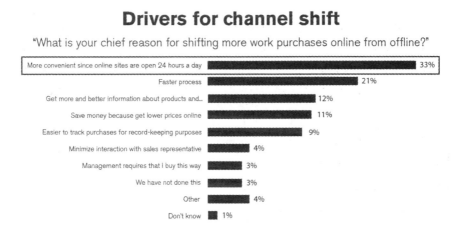

| | |
|---|---|
| More convenient since online sites are open 24 hours a day | 33% |
| Faster process | 21% |
| Get more and better information about products and... | 12% |
| Save money because get lower prices online | 11% |
| Easier to track purchases for record-keeping purposes | 9% |
| Minimize interaction with sales representative | 4% |
| Management requires that I buy this way | 3% |
| We have not done this | 3% |
| Other | 4% |
| Don't know | 1% |

Base: 140 B2B online buyers

*More business purchases are shifting online*[2]

Considerable business activity is booming across multiple channels, or shifting to digital commerce outright. In turn, business processes are shifting online, notably for self-service models for E-Commerce, partner commerce and mobile commerce. A growing number of businesses are finding it necessary to coordinate activities and information between the online and offline worlds (i.e., bridge in-person

---

[1]   Business Wire, Introducing Amazon Business: Everything You Love About Amazon, For Your Business, April 28, 2015

[2]   Source: Q4 2015 Forrester/Internet Retailer B2B Buy-Side Survey

interactions with the business conducted or over the phone or via the Internet). By having in integrated end-to-end Quote-to-Cash system, the data across the channels can be captured and you will gain a single view of the customer's journey through the buying cycle.

> Digital channels and E-Commerce are a must in an economy where we purchase a growing number of subscriptions and services.

Though it's challenging enough in its own right to get multi-channel sales correct, it's even more complicated when companies sell through indirect channels (e.g., resellers, distributors) and lose their main line of visibility to end customers. Additionally, organizations must often incentivize third parties to push their products in the form of commissions, rebates and discounts—all additional transactional details about your customer that must be tracked and executed accurately.

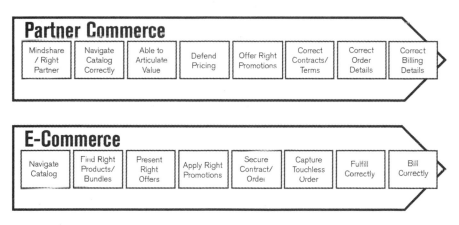

*Business concerns extend across channels*

This trend affects a broad range of industry sectors, including manufacturing, life sciences and financial services, in addition to industries long focused on E-Commerce, like retail, software and media. For example, a field service subcontractor can now use just a mobile device to quickly find and purchase parts online for oil-rig equipment from preferred partners. All the discounts and approvals are automatically executed, without any human interactions between the subcontractor and the vendor. Even when customers buy directly from a vendor, they increasingly do so using multiple channels in the process. A buyer might start researching a product by visiting a dealership to see it in person, conduct online research to gather reviews from existing customers, and then order the product via the vendor's website. Getting insight into the customer's journey across all your channels is very important.

Here's another example. A realty business looking to purchase a sales automation package could first network on LinkedIn to create a short list of vendors and then visit their sites. Because of its industry-specific needs, the realty business may also want to tap into a vendor's partners. To that end, it makes a call into a vendor's call center for information on local partners with experience customizing and deploying realty solutions. The realty business then may want to schedule an in-person meeting to meet the potential partner. From end to end, the prospect journey could span social media, a standard website, an E-Commerce storefront, a call center as well as the classic sales meeting before the sales cycle is even kicked off.

Clearly it's vital for businesses to grasp and support this shift to digital channels: they need to have insights about all the customer touchpoints with their brands, products, and pricing across all channels. In other words, they must ensure a continuum of interactions and seamless experience across channels. However, in most cases—even though many companies have already sold through multiple channels for decades—multi-channel selling can be disjointed, leading to missed opportunities resulting in revenue leakage, cannibalization of products and margin erosion. The fact is that few organizations have been able to coordinate omni-channel efforts to maximize the customer experience, as well as company profits. Unfortunately, it is more of an exception than a rule.

While companies suffer in such cases, so do their customers. In fact, according to research by McKinsey, on average, a B2B customer regularly uses six different interaction channels on the path to purchase, and nearly 65% end up frustrated by inconsistent experiences.[1]

No matter how customers engage with the brand—whether directly in person, or online via a company or partner website accessed from a desktop or mobile phone—it's irrelevant to customers how the purchase is enabled behind the scenes. Customers simply want to complete their purchase and access the product or service as quickly and easily as possible. In this way, successful omni-channel selling comes down to dramatically improving the ease of doing business for customers in ways that make financial sense for the company.

Andy Hoar, a Principal Analyst with Forrester Research, says that one of the key elements of an omni-channel, world-class B2B digital-centric buying experience is a frictionless buying process. According to the First-ever Guide to B2B E-Commerce published by Internet Retailer magazine, "…succeeding at B2B E-commerce is… about figuring out how to help business customers find the full range of products they need, saving them time and helping them to do their jobs better as purchasing managers as well as users of the seller's products."[2]

E-Commerce has become one of the most powerful channels in the multi-channel paradigm. Other than enabling the degree of responsiveness and availability that customers demand, E-Commerce puts more power in the hands of customers and partners. Consider these findings from surveys of B2B buyers:

- 74% research at least half of their purchases online[3]

- 30% complete at least half of their work purchases online, and that's expected to rise to 56% by 2017 [4]

---

[1]   McKinsey Quarterly, Do you really understand how your business customers buy?, February 2015

[2]   Internet Retailer, First-ever B2B Guide to E-commerce, 2015 Edition

[3]   Forrester, US B2B eCommerce Forecast: 2015 To 2020, April 2, 2015

[4]   Ibid

- Almost 75% say buying from a website is more convenient than buying from a sales representative[1]

- 93% say they prefer buying online rather than from a salesperson once they've decided what to buy[2]

As a result, customer data is becoming the most critical asset for the majority of companies. And that's why the success of a multi- or omni-channel strategy comes down to connecting and mining the various information and system silos that enable the underlying business processes. Underpinning this with an integrated end-to-end Quote-to-Cash system, you will have a complete picture of the customer journey. An E-Commerce system itself is insufficient. Hoar advises "Tomorrow's winning B2B sellers will be those that respond faster, act more nimbly and offer differentiated value to B2B buyers." And that requires them to "design systems that can handle complex order management requirements across multiple touchpoints."[3] By doing this, companies can enrich the customer experience and drive tremendous value from customer insights in terms of future strategy.

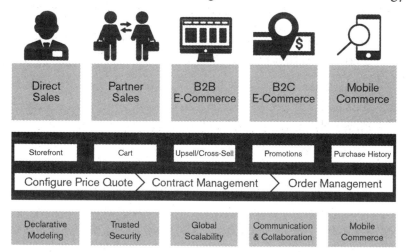

*Businesses must support multi-channel sales*
*for all products, on a single platform*

---

[1]  Forrester, Death Of A (B2B) Salesman, April 13, 2015

[2]  Ibid

[3]  Internet Retailer, First-ever B2B Guide to E-commerce, 2015 Edition

At the same time, B2B companies need to accommodate dynamic changes in their omni-channel strategies and technologies (think consumerization of IT, the critical importance of the customer experience, the rise of mobile commerce, and the return of partner commerce, to name a few). And in today's competitive climate, they need to do so while ensuring rapid innovation and fast time to market in the most cost-effective way possible, such as by outsourcing staffing and technological infrastructure.

All this means that the most important tool for a successful omni-channel strategy is a robust E-Commerce platform with a strong and integrated Quote-to-Cash system underpinning the E-Commerce platform. But even the strongest platform needs the support of a strong ecosystem to fill in gaps, nurture innovation as well as to service specific industries.

> The mandate for businesses is to hide the underlying complexity of omni-channel sales while strategically consolidating and capitalizing on the information collected across channels. They must:
>
> • Orchestrate the interactions and transactions across channels into a seamless experience
>
> • Collect and combine the information that is generated via the individual interactions and transactions across channels and make it available to all stakeholders throughout the organization

For example, when it comes to the Apttus Quote-to-Cash platform, our partners provide additional capabilities like electronic signatures for contracts. Other platforms—such as Oracle and Microsoft—rely on partners to support other end-to-end processes, enable analytics that help capitalize on Big Data flowing through the platform, and more. Additionally, a modern platform needs to be able to handle enormous growth in complexity, business models and processes.

The platform approach and this complexity are key reasons the cloud plays such a significant role in helping companies address their toughest business process issues. It's much easier for a cloud-based platform provider than an on-premise solution vendor to cultivate a healthy, thriving ecosystem. And it's much faster and more cost-effective to tap into a cloud platform for scalability. And investors have recognized this too. As a result, cloud application providers have been the star investments commanding very high valuations.

The entire E-Commerce infrastructure is oriented around a scalable platform so that organizations can drastically simplify how to do business. Of note is the connection with back-office data (e.g., inventory status) from systems such as ERP, which connects customer purchase data, product catalogues, and purchase history from all channels inside the CRM tool. This is where Quote-to-Cash systems become the key because they allow visibility of the data connection between CRM and ERP. E-Commerce integrated with a CRM tool provides unparalleled visibility into the customer relationship, but it does not provide the transaction data that is also needed to get a single view of the customer. When underpinned with a Quote-to-Cash system, customer data is fully integrated to provide end-to-end transparency across channels, product lines, and customer segments, enabling companies to analyze buyer behavior patterns, detect trends, and remove barriers to sale. It allows companies to focus their resources and increase the value of more complex, high-touch transactions.

The cloud-based element is critical for another reason. Consider the classic—static—distribution model as shown below. It's simply not designed to support the demands and preferences of today's buyers who traverse multiple channels as they research, purchase, and consume products and services.

Enterprises need to prioritize on initiatives and software platforms that rationalize technology assets, ensure consistency across customer touch points, and deliver the necessary flexibility for changing functionality as business strategies and processes change.

Companies need a cloud-based platform to scale across the proliferation of channels and deliver the fast, accurate, frictionless experience that customers expect. Only with a cloud-based E-Commerce solution coupled with a Quote-to-Cash system that eliminates system silos and seamlessly integrates with back-end systems, can companies deliver a single customer experience regardless of touchpoint.

## Traditional B2B Ecosystem

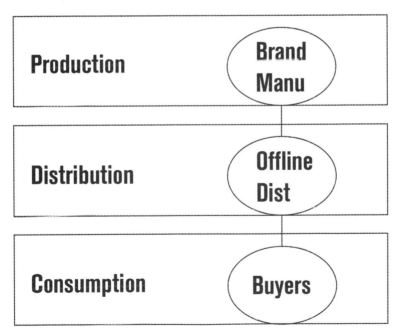

*Traditional B2B ecosystems*
*do not support today's buying preferences*

# New B2B Ecosystem

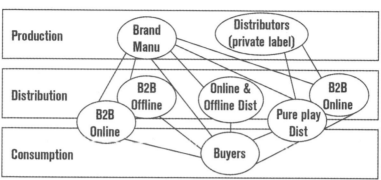

*New B2B ecosystems support commerce
across channels for a seamless buying experience*

Some companies have tried to enable multi-channel sales but failed because they chose a solution that was unable to scale. Others realize they must change their business model and support multi-channel business in order to avoid becoming obsolete. It's all about a race to stay relevant with customers, and those that are adopting and enabling E-Commerce with integrated Quote-to-Cash system are succeeding.

One company in the bond credit rating business needed to support clients who expected a high-touch experience when signing contracts in person but also wanted the convenience of seeing the end result online. To ensure a seamless continuum of interactions and deliver a consumer-grade experience, it needed to integrate four customer touchpoints, 12 functional areas, and more than 40 cross-functional business process work streams. It did so by developing a self-service customer portal that provides customers with a simple app-like experience and allows them to complete their contract process in minutes instead of hours or days. And though it is invisible to customers, an integrated Quote-to-Cash process on the back-end processes enables all this front-end functionality.

> Omni-channel E-Commerce is a great galvanizer of the quote, contract and revenue workflow. When it's cloud-based, companies can "own" the omni-channel process and drive down costs and time to great advantage. That's because it enables them to orchestrate the most complex strategies, including new product introductions, pricing and product promotions, regional product launches and more.

When it comes to partner commerce, vendors typically struggle to ensure consistency for the end customer, make accurate payouts on rebates and promotions, and gain insight, via partners, into what's happening in the market. But when a company's partners are selling products and/or services via their website on behalf of the vendor, the Quote-to-Cash system needs to be tied into it all. Manufacturers, suppliers and vendors gain superior visibility into activities across the extended value chain of partners and distributors. They can see what is being sold, at what price, due to what promotions, and to whom.

This helps connect the dots between agreements, purchases, rebates and promotions claimed by partners and customers. As a result, organizations can improve the way they sell to customers and interact with and manage partners. In fact, they can better understand who is and isn't actively selling, and track trends in regional and even test markets.

Even the certification and onboarding of partners is simplified because of the electronic linkage between Quote-to-Cash-related and E-Commerce-related systems and processes. Vendors can more easily distribute and manage partner-specific leads, and handle deal registration and contracts. Moreover, because they make it easy to navigate their product portfolio, pricing, and promotions, they can boost their partners' effectiveness. All of these capabilities, in combination with the dramatically increased visibility into partner activities, tip the balance of power back in favor of the supplier/vendor.

Companies that excel in today's omni-channel world are those with tightly integrated channel strategies that treat customers like a pipeline of revenue. By streamlining the E-Commerce process for their customers, these businesses have measurable business impact by being easy to do business with.

Consider how one global leader in mailing solutions wanted to create an omni-channel solution to offer a seamless experience for customers of its communications and shipping services. Previously, its sales reps had struggled with a cumbersome order entry process due to a large and complex product list and the use of multiple sales systems. It took both internal sales reps and partners a long time to navigate through multiple catalogs and sites, and they struggled to find what they wanted because they "got lost in the catalog." That had led to quoting and order delays. Plus, there was always the risk of more serious issues presenting themselves, such as different versions of pricing or product information being published and used by different sales teams, partners and websites. That lead to errors, delays and revisions to quotes and orders.

# Business Impact:
# Streamlined E-Commerce Process

| Streamlined E-Commerce Process | Increase Revenues | **Increased Revenue & Margins**<br><br>Increase quoting accuracy over 90%<br>Increase in customer face time 25-50%<br>Sales productivity up from 9% to 25%<br>25-50% reduction in engineering time<br>Special pricing requests yield 100%+ improvement in sales |
|---|---|---|
| | Grow and Maintain Margins | |
| | Reducing the Cost of Sales | **Reducing Costs**<br><br>Reduction in order cycle from 17-33 hrs to 30 minutes<br>30-60% reduction in cost per lead<br>15% savings in engineering sales support<br>Avg 20% increases utilization ratio of mfg centers<br>Order re-work reduced from 15% to 2%<br>233% avg increase in cross-sells<br>10% reduction in warranty costs |
| | More Effective Utilization of Assets | |
| | Reducing Accts. Receivables & Costs to Collect | **Improved Financial performance**<br><br>95% reduction in order completion cost<br>65% reduction in order cycle times<br>50-60% reduction in Days Sales Outstanding (DSOs)<br>30% reduction in accounts receivables<br>2x avg increases in inventory terms<br>25% reduction on cost of sales |

By integrating and automating its end-to-end Quote-to-Cash process, the company was able to create a customizable user interface and storefront integrated with a single product catalog. This enabled the company to put the power into its customers' hands by automating the quoting process. As a result, the company was able to globally scale its multi-channel sales while also supporting those on mobile devices. Specifically, the company evolved from a single product catalog to one propagated across a multi-channel environment, enabling an entirely new business model. In the process, it secured 19% market share and expanded business to 220 cities.

Though it's no small undertaking to put in place the necessary strategy and technology for omni-channel selling and digital commerce, the writing is on the wall: adapt and thrive or ignore these trends and risk obsolescence.

To prepare for the omni-channel shift, companies should reevaluate the positioning of products and how their customers actually go about making evaluations and purchases. We recommend they follow a four step action plan to update and improve their understanding of product sales by channel, the buyer's journeys, pivotal moments within channels and potential sources of channel conflict.

1. **Evaluate Product Portfolio for Complexity:** Categorize products based on sophistication and suitability for specific channels. A big concern is the amount of assistance required to educate customers and to actually close sales. Standalone, discrete products and bundles are commonly sold online, either directly from or through partners (like buying a power drill or a mobile phone plan). Now, however, it's possible to enable online product configuration, for example. This opens up new opportunities for selling higher value offerings on the Web while reducing selling costs. Companies need to carefully define the points in buying cycles when assistance is clearly needed to move a sale along. At the same time, recognize that certain products

and sales will always involve professional sale people, like the procurement of heavy equipment such as elevators.

# Spectrum of Product Complexity

Companies should categorize how their products and services map to the spectrum of product complexity. Simpler products tend to lend themselves to strictly online purchases, while more complex products may require a mix of selling approaches and channels.

| | Salable Items | Catalog Selections | Configurable products | Complex Configurations | Complex Solutions |
|---|---|---|---|---|---|
| Definition | Standalone, discrete products that are easy to purchase with any assistance | Basic attributes, accessories and other choices that can be selected easily without help | Major components & intermediate assemblies that can be changed as well as options and parts | Product bundles comprising extension variation in components, involving configurations | Solutions that receive considerable tailoring for engineer-to-order and configure-to-order deals |
| Examples | Retail goods, apparel | Electronics, appliances | Small machines | Commercial vehicles | Medical equipment |
| | | | | | |

Simple ———————————————————————————————————————————— Complex

2. **Map Customer Journeys:** Trace customer-buying behaviors and anticipate how channels are traversed, from brick-and-mortar to online, or partner to direct, to understand customer preferences. For example, customers who buy products from an equipment provider like Bobcat will likely browse products online before visiting a dealer to complete a purchase. They may get an extended warranty from the same dealer, but renew the warranties online. Spare parts and accessories may be purchased from a local shop. Understanding commonalities in journeys within target customer segments creates significant advantages in prioritizing sales and marketing programs for different channels. Ideally, vendors can capitalize on trends in customer preferences to expand or promote lower-cost-to-serve options, like reordering online instead of using a call center (which can be 90% more cost-effective).

3. **Match Buying Phases with Channels:** Look at key process steps for marketing, sales and servicing, to determine "best channel" by buying stage, to raise mindshare, lower the

cost-to-serve and drive sales. Ideally, vendors can identify "moments of truth" by buying stage (e.g., discovery, education, evaluation, etc.) along with channel preference. This includes determining when mindshare is consistently captured, when customer interest turns serious and when an intent to make a purchase becomes clear. Understanding such moments will help any effort to increase conversion rates. Look at how prospects and customers are browsing and researching products, their use of online reviews, when or if they solicit information from live representatives, where they make purchases, and how they reorder products or renew relationships. A big issue is uncovering buying activity in the early stages of a purchase (often a majority of legwork in making a decision has already gone undetected), as well as advancing prospects from researching products online to channels best suited to close deals.

4. **Proactively Address Channel Conflict:** Put in place the right communication, education program and ground rules to curtail uncertainty, anger and doubt among partners and sales. Partners will need to be reassured that they are not being undercut. Salespeople will fear that their territory will be encroached upon if customers don't go directly through them, and that their chances at making quota will be hurt. In both cases, highlight the value of omni-channel strategies in improving lead quality for both partners and internal sales. Similarly, highlight how the information from different channels will strengthen their hand in accelerating sales cycles. In addition, consider counting reordering activity towards sales during transition periods, when customers are getting shifted to online channels.

Businesses that can skillfully manage the omni-channel experience will dramatically increase their competitiveness, revenues and profits, while those who fail to adopt, run a risk of seriously being left behind by the competition. And companies that rely on separate, siloed systems to enable the Quote-to-Cash process will end up with inconsistent data about customers, including the customer journey, quotes, contracts, orders and more. That leads to mistakes and confusion that frustrates customers, driving them away to organizations that do have seamless touchpoints with their customers. Only an integrated, automated Quote-to-Cash process is capable of capturing all customer data and transactions to enable a seamless, end-to-end experience for the customer.

Done right, omni-channel sales can prove revolutionary for a business. Today many companies are using the cloud and incorporating E-Commerce (i.e., digital) to "create competitive advantage through new offerings, new business models, and new customer, supplier, and distributor relationships."[1] But the key is to support this with an integrated Quote-to-Cash system and process. With this, organizations become a catalyst for new revenues and make themselves much more customer friendly and easier to do business with.

---

[1] Forbes, Transform Or Die: IDC's Top Technology Predictions For 2016, November 10, 2015

# 6 Quote-to-Cash Across the Value Chain

**B**usiness relationships are obviously the most vital link underpinning the success of every organization. The world's most competitive companies harness and orchestrate business relationships into value chains that scale to meet customer demands. That's why one needs to rethink and maximize relationships beyond the company's four walls.

Selling in the modern world is no longer a matter of a sales rep calling directly on a customer. In today's global, omni-channel business world, organizations are increasingly connecting with entities throughout the value chain, from partners to customers. The world we live in today is social, mobile and virtual—and all the technologies exist to enable companies to better harness the customer experience. According to Forrester Consulting, "Excellent customer engagement requires the right omni-channel strategy, partner ecosystem, and technology infrastructure to meet buyers' expectations. Creating a consistent, high-quality customer experience across any channel entails more than just putting point solutions in place. Mastering digital strategies to actively engage customers requires a focused business technology agenda that puts the customer in the center, a culture of constant iteration and analysis, and (usually) support from a partner ecosystem to help fill capability gaps and speed time-to-market."[1]

In this way, companies are operating in a hub-and-spoke model, where the company is in the middle as the producer of the product or service. The organization is then surrounded by all the elements

---

[1] Forrester Consulting, Mastering Omni-Channel B2B Customer Engagement, October 2015

that make up its wider ecosystem. This wider ecosystem can include channels (such as E-Commerce), along with distributors, suppliers, retailers, custom brokers, logistics service providers, and partners offering such things as warranties and value-added services. These are the "spokes" that enable customers to engage with the company and purchase and consume its offerings.

> A company's Quote-to-Cash process must accommodate and fa-
> cilitate each and every point of engagement in the hub and spoke.
> Customer touch technologies such as social, mobile and virtual
> technologies can greatly facilitate this while giving the company
> full visibility into all this engagement and consumption.

Some still refer to this as the "supply chain," but recognize that the chain has grown to include more parties than ever before. Deloitte characterizes this as 'supply chains' evolving into 'value webs,' "which span and connect whole ecosystems of suppliers and collaborators."[1] It's well worth getting this right. Deloitte contends that, "Properly activated, these value webs can be more effective on multiple dimensions—reducing costs, improving service levels, mitigating risks of disruption, and delivering feedback-fueled learning and innovation."[2] That's important considering that companies like yours are under constant pressure to boost order accuracy, use speed to gain a competitive edge, and find ways to make every supplier, distributor and service interaction count.

Just what does it take to activate these value webs—or to achieve a competitive edge with a value chain? As Aberdeen Group explains, "The omni-channel world we live in requires online, cloud-ready orchestration of events and activities across an increasingly multi-party end-to-end supply chain."[3] The ability to accommodate buyers' needs in today's digital landscape requires more than a simple tweaking of

---

[1]

[2]  Ibid

[3]  Aberdeen Group, Profitable Supply Chain Execution with Customer- and Event-Driven Optimization, January 2016

a company's internal processes; it requires total transformation of the way they go from Quote-to-Cash.

Most companies base their Quote-to-Cash process on a series of fixed, separate processes that—theoretically—run sequentially. These processes are usually only loosely integrated through management oversight. In fact, in the not-so-distant past, companies could operate fairly successfully even though their value chain comprised disjointed parts. That's because a growing economy and less competitive markets allowed them to pull other levers—such as tapping into remote, low-cost manufacturing, rationalizing their supplier base, and reducing inventories—to make up for the weaknesses. Essentially, yesterday's economy allowed companies to absorb and tolerate the gaps in their value chains.

However, in a compressed economy, companies don't have this luxury. Today's customers expect rapid response to their inquiries, a smooth purchasing process, and fast delivery of products and services. To succeed in today's volatile and dynamic business environment, companies must enable different business functions and parties in the extended value chain to plan, monitor, and respond simultaneously. Simply put, the cadence of change and continual quality improvement customers want across all industries has forced the many functions of value chains to merge into a single, unified organization. The bottom line is that value chains are getting flattened across all industries as customers express much greater urgency for higher quality products and services and much greater responsiveness than ever before. To that end, companies need to enable the entire value chain of separate companies to act as one, single, contiguous entity sharing insight and intelligence predicated on analytics.

That's where a cloud-enabled Quote-to-Cash system comes into play. Quote-to-Cash strategies enabled with scalable, secure and globally available cloud platforms are making it possible for organizations to move beyond myopic, inward-driven measures of efficiency to embrace new customer driven-metrics. Put another way, a cloud-based

Quote-to-Cash system gives your company the opportunity to inject its innate intelligence and knowledge into every sales situation. While on-premise systems can also help do this, cloud-based ones are much more flexible, quicker to roll out, easier to customize, and often more rapidly and widely adopted by those in the extended value chain.

Forward-thinking manufacturers are orchestrating about 80% or more of their supplier network activity outside their four walls, using Big Data and cloud-based technologies to overcome the constraints of legacy Enterprise Resource Planning (ERP) and Supply Chain Management (SCM) systems. For companies whose business models are based on rapid product lifecycles and speed, legacy ERP systems are a bottleneck. Designed to deliver order, shipment and transactional data, these systems can't provide the flexibility to meet the challenges associated with today's extended value chains. Moreover, they don't enable more complex supplier networks that recognize the value of knowledge sharing and collaboration over just completing transactions.

Consider findings from Aberdeen Group's research: "From the customer or demand-group of processes, the cloud-based leaders are better connected across processes from order to deliver/service/cash."[1] In fact, Aberdeen argues that advanced automation and cloud-connected interoperability are key to profitable execution in today's world. With such capabilities in hand, companies can "better synchronize profitability and services levels across customer cost-to-serve, products, and omni-channel logistics flows."[2]

As businesses see their networks expand, an integrated, automated Quote-to-Cash process enables them to integrate their processes with those of their partners and suppliers. In effect, they can orchestrate all customer-focused activities and maintain needed visibility and insight across all channels and the entire value chain. This is critical as companies spread their operations across the globe and operate

---

[1]  Aberdeen Group, Profitable Supply Chain Execution with Customer- and Event-Driven Optimization, January 2016

[2]  Ibid

within increasingly complex supply—or value—chains. The outcome—and payoff—of all that synchronization with those across the value chain is greater speed and order accuracy and higher levels of customer satisfaction. At a time when it's harder than ever to cultivate customer loyalty, every interaction counts.

Some would argue that the velocity of information flow across the value chain is a key determinant of success in today's world. A study completed by AMR Research in conjunction with Webster University, on behalf of an Apttus client, illustrates the impact. The study found a correlation between operational performance and integration of geographically diverse and distributed order management hubs. The greater the integration, the higher the percentage of perfect orders, transaction velocity and inventory turns. That's not all: at the 95% confidence interval, the study found that the tighter the integration of production centers with suppliers, support centers and distributors, the lower the percentage of order errors. This in turn further improved perfect order performance and order velocity.

Fortunately, current technologies make it possible to unite the disparate parts of the value chain so they are more tightly integrated and can better share information. In essence, cloud computing flattens the value chain, enabling organizations to truly operate from a customer-centric perspective. Per Accenture, cloud computing makes this possible by:

- Empowering organizations to accommodate and respond more quickly to supply chain disruptions
- Enabling data to flow across the entire value chain, powering actionable insights
- Allowing businesses to more flexibly and quickly produce or deliver customized products and services
- Enabling the real-time collaboration and visibility necessary to support today's business strategies[1]

---

[1] Accenture, Supply chain management in the cloud: How can cloud-based computing make supply chains more competitive?, 2014

And an integrated Quote-to-Cash process is the underpinning for this smoothly flowing value chain. That's because the automation of the Quote-to-Cash process allows companies to fluidly connect their critical data and processes. As the single link between top-line growth, bottom-line results and customer satisfaction, Quote-to-Cash relies on the collective intelligence of the enterprise—and all parties in the value chain. Integrated, automated Quote-to-Cash featuring sanctioned quotes, workflows, contract templates and intelligent guidance empowers sales reps to assemble and price optimal deals on their own, from any location at any time. That means any party within the value chain is empowered to accurately and quickly move deals through the pipeline from opportunity to close.

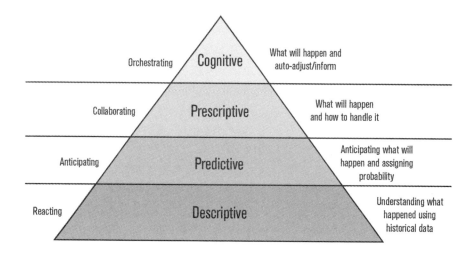

*The ultimate goal is to move up the Intelligence Capability Pyramid, from reacting based on an understanding of historical data to orchestrating quotes and contracts by automatically adjusting terms based on an understanding of what will happen as a result.*

The impact of accurate quotes, proposals, contracts and orders is a better customer experience and translates into more revenue for your company. With a single process and data stream across the entire value chain, companies can easily and accurately measure effectiveness and take steps to optimize.

Take the example of a leading manufacturer of heavy machinery. This company's success hinges greatly on enabling effective sales across its extremely diverse dealer base, which ranges from mom-and-pop shops all the way to large corporations and represents a wide spectrum of sales maturity. It calls upon a plethora of systems—including ERP—to drive its operations and that of its extended value chain. Key to this is its use of an automated, integrated Quote-to-Cash process in the cloud that evens the playing field by enabling a consistent, high-quality online buying experience across the distributor network.

By standardizing in this way, the company reduces the potential for order errors and in turn drives up order accuracy. Quote-to-Cash Intelligence gives it visibility into all sales and E-Commerce-related activity and performance, and in particular the impact of greater quote and order accuracy. In this case, Quote-to-Cash Intelligence acts as a unifying agent across all the value chain elements.

# 7 Quote-to-Cash
## Revolutionizing Business Across Industries

Now we shall take a closer look at how Quote-to-Cash affects certain industries. Although the fundamental process is essentially the same for most industries, the subtleties and differences in the details can make these processes very different and require slightly different approaches across industries.

However, like most organizations, you may still be hesitant to take the step of actually putting such significant changes in place. Resistance to change in the business world can be explained from many angles, but here are three that often surface:

- The perception that transformation carries with it greater risk than the risk of staying with the status quo

- People lack the confidence to spearhead change without proof that it's worth the risk

- Fear of being the first in the industry to implement a transformational approach to a process involving customers and partners

The earlier chapters in this book should have made it clear that the risk of not adapting to the new world pressures and updating the Quote-to-Cash systems and processes is far greater than the risk of transformation. As illustrated in previous chapters, a disjointed Quote-to-Cash process actually undermines efforts to drive the best possible business results. Simply put, it's impossible to close deals as quickly as possible, ensure the most favorable contract terms, go above and beyond in satisfying customers, and record profitable revenues faster than ever, without an integrated, automated Quote-to-Cash process. In fact, it's not possible to launch and support the new business models and extended value chains required to succeed in today's global economy without a seamless Quote-to-Cash process. The good news is that numerous companies across industries have already "crossed the chasm" and have automated and modernized their Quote-to-Cash process. In other words, you don't need to break new ground in pursuing this transformation—you simply have to follow in the footsteps of those that have already succeeded by doing so. Let's explore a few real-world examples.

## Industrial Manufacturing: Enabling an Online Partner Portal

To keep pace with the increasingly digitized nature of today's world, one of the world's leading large-scale manufacturers of machinery and heavy equipment and related services developed a vision to revolutionize its industry. It executed on this vision by launching a comprehensive self-service marketplace that enabled partners to engage customers with self-service touch, specifically E-Commerce. The goal was to streamline the purchase process for customers, partners, and dealers with a model that resembles the browse-shop-compare-buy retail experience, as much as possible. Rather than having to navigate multiple sales channels, customers are able to find and buy products and services with ease through an online E-Commerce site. A major difference between this and traditional E-Commerce is that products and services are developed and offered by third parties in the company's extended ecosystem and could conceivably even include competitors in the near future. This innovative industrial manufacturer is betting big on this initiative, estimating significant revenue growth by growing its marketplace into a default destination of comprehensive solutions for its customers and prospects.

To make this vision a reality, the company had to develop and support an entirely new way of doing business. This revolved around centralizing the purchase flow process in order to enable:

- Revenue capture from both customers and companies that offer services via the platform

- Users to find, buy, activate, deactivate and provide feedback on solutions provided

- Third-party companies and service providers to communicate the availability and value of their solutions

- Service providers to configure and bundle solutions and pricing

And the company had to enable this all online—a dramatic shift for an industrial manufacturer.

It found its solution by leveraging a CRM tool as a technology platform for its marketplace, and using Apttus to drive the Quote-to-Cash and E-Commerce experience while seamlessly feeding transactional and fulfillment data into its back-end SAP ERP instance. The Apttus solution makes it possible for this industrial manufacturer to address all its needs in the purchase flow process. Even better, with an integrated, automated Quote-to-Cash process in place, it is:

- Recommending the best products to customers, partners, and dealers

- Efficiently catering to customers' unique needs when it comes to configuring, pricing, and quoting

- Enabling fast, accurate reordering

- Automatically managing renewals driving higher customer retention rates

## Common Manufacturing Industry Challenges

- Product quoting and configuration mistakes are extremely costly

- Time-consuming quoting process due to large reliance on selling through partners

- Long sales cycles because deals require coordination and collaboration between sales, engineers and sometimes partners

## High-tech Manufacturing: Preventing Revenue Leakage in the Distribution Channel

A multinational technology company was experiencing a high degree of inefficiency and manual replication of data in processing timely and accurate rebate and other channel payments for its retail distribution partners. An ever-growing set of products and programs posed a dramatically increasing challenge to already burdened teams and processes—a major concern in an industry where rebate errors can range between 6-8% requests. One underlying issue was cumbersome collaboration between marketing, finance and legal to set up program budgets, pricing and rebate templates and guidelines. Complicating matters was a manual and expensive process for receiving, verifying, and auditing proof of sales from these retailers. Moreover, the company's manual rebate management process provided no visibility into pricing guidance and exceptions. With rebate calculations handled completely via spreadsheet, employees ran the risk of not keeping up and making errors that affected partner satisfaction. Perhaps more importantly, over time the inability to flag duplicate rebate requests and previous payments could have led to the company paying out unnecessary rebates and taking a revenue hit.

To address this process gap, the company chose to take advantage of its investment in its CRM tool and implement a solution that leveraged core customer, channel and product data. This Quote-to-Cash system enabled it to control all aspects of the channel incentives program from planning, forecasting and contracts to payment and reconciliation.

## Life Sciences: Adeptly Managing Sales Across an Extended Value Chain

A global manufacturer of medical devices and supplies is up against the same forces impacting others in its industry: tight regulation, growing cost pressures, and the influence of physician preferences. To sell in this environment, the company's sales force must negotiate sales contracts directly with a range of entities, from hospitals and managed care organizations to integrated delivery networks. And they are usually offering and selling complex solution bundles with highly variable pricing and using combinations of discounts and rebates as well as other channel incentives. This is a kind of complexity unseen in many other industries.

The company's siloed, homegrown contract and pricing applications weren't able to support these complex needs. Just as important, its sales reps lacked end-to-end visibility of the Quote-to-Cash process within its organization and across the extended value chain. In particular, they struggled to ascertain buyers' affiliations with third-party purchasing entities, along with eligibility for tiered prices tied to purchase commitments from hospital and provider customers. As a result, sales reps didn't always quote using the correct price, creating potential for revenue leakage and customer disputes.

Recognizing the need to evolve to a more modern, flexible Quote-to-Cash solution that could be easily integrated with its CRM and ERP systems, the company deployed Apttus. By integrating and automating its Quote-to-Cash process, it was able to accommodate its complicated, ramped-pricing and group-purchasing sales models. The real value is in how this modernization impacted the business.

With an integrated, automated Quote-to-Cash process, the company has been able to:

- Ensure price accuracy in the quoting and contracting process
- Drastically accelerate the sales cycle and quote approval time
- Keep rampant discounting in check
- Facilitate more cross- and upsells by recommending appropriate warranties and disposables be included in quotes
- Activate and renew contracts in time
- Propagate contract pricing and rebate terms to downstream quoting and rebate processes in a timely manner

## Common Life Sciences Industry Challenges

- Managing complex pricing and bundling strategies across buying groups, distributors and hospitals
- Revenue leakage due to overlapping contracts, contract non-compliance, and inaccuracies in rebate computation, overpayments and disputes

## Telecommunications: Streamlined Quoting Leads to More Deals and Revenue

A global communications, hosting, cloud and IT services company— relied on disjointed Configure-Price-Quote (CPQ) solutions to handle its complex product configuration and pricing needs. Like many communications service providers, it offers standalone products and services, as well as multi-level bundles (think triple- and quad-play offerings). And like others in its industry that call upon disparate CPQ applications, it faced many classic problems:

- Delays in responding to prospective customers, resulting in lost deals

- Errors in quotes requiring extensive rework and manual intervention
- Inability to handle the complexity in catalog and quoting requirements
- Long ramp-up times for new sales reps

To enable faster, more consistent product configurations, error-free quotes, and a more intuitive self-service user experience for its sales reps and partners, the company chose to replace its fragmented CPQ systems with Apttus. By implementing Apttus solutions, it equipped its sales reps with an advanced toolset that accelerates onboarding, streamlines the configuration and quoting process, and enables better customer service. The integrated, automated process has proven so successful that the company is working with Apttus to set up a solution that enabled it to sell across its entire catalog of network, cloud, hosting and IT solutions. As a result, it was able to:

- Easily handle complex configurations of bundles, subscriptions and renewals
- Optimize configuration, availability and pricing of complex connectivity offerings based on location or installation site characteristics such as availability of fiber channels
- Guide selling based on customers' needs and current services

## Common Communications Industry Challenges

- Orchestrate and provision services throughout the customer lifecycle, from service initiation to service usage, monitoring and service management and service termination.

- Most telco orders/service requests are Moves, Adds, Changes and Disconnects (MACD), meaning they are modifications to existing services. Because inventory is constantly changing, it can be challenging to handle these requests and tie expenses back to the appropriate cost centers.

## Financial Services: Succeeding with a New Business Model

When a major financial institution was on the path to achieve a competitive edge for its investment management services business, it took a multi-pronged approach. This included repositioning its brand and evolving digitally to realize radical gains in operating efficiency. After all, its main revenue stream was driven through an external broker network, yet the company's reliance on six separate systems for quoting and proposals undermined efforts to run a modern business. More specifically, this use of outdated means resulted in:

- Inability for the company's sales teams to be more consultative in their approach

- Incapacity for third-party brokers to build proposals on-site with clients

- Mistakes and reworks due to inaccurate pricing

- Critical quoting delays that threatened deal closure

- Lack of up-to-date deal information tied to client opportunities from the broker network that made it difficult to assess the impact of new and bundled products, fee models and add-on services

- Rogue discounting, which eroded margins

Building on its existing cloud-based investment in its CRM tool, this financial institution deployed Apttus solutions to enable an end-to-end Quote-to-Cash process across its organization and broker network. Through the Apttus solution, the organization now easily onboards partners. Additionally, they can define deal parameters by setting rules based on discount levels, product status, customer history and operational constraints. At the same time, because of the unique X-Author capability within Apttus, sales reps can use Microsoft Excel while in their CRM tool, ensuring all reps are working from the same data and rules.

The results speak for themselves. With an integrated, automated process in place, the organization was empowered to:

- Change the composition and playbook for partners so they could focus on speedy execution, solution differentiation, and value instead of pricing and discounting

- Restructure its entire sales team and dramatically scale the organization

- Quickly adapt to market needs, easily adding, revising or deleting retirement funds—without a single line of code or the need for IT involvement

- Evolve from a dedicated back-office team to a self-service model, reallocating headcount from six sales operations staff down to one

- Eliminated the 2-3 day lead time previously required for proposals

- Reduced time to create a proposal from 2 hours to 15 minutes on average

- Achieved better margins by stopping rogue discounting

Remote sales reps and brokers now create dynamic proposals for prospective clients—both individuals and employers offering 401ks—in a live environment, working from one common system. Using a live portal, employers and employees can now assess risk and reallocate funds on a real-time basis.

## Common Financial Services Industry Challenges

- Disruptive, digitized competitors are attracting a new breed of customers

- Millions spent to prevent data incongruence and non-compliance across disconnected systems—all in the midst of rapidly and continually changing standards and laws

- Balancing expense management with innovation and restructuring

## Institutional Asset and Wealth Management Firm: Satisfying the Demand for Self-Service

Like many of today's businesses, a major wealth and asset management firm uses multiple applications (35) to manage its main business process (end-to-end wealth management) and to sell a huge portfolio of over 400 products and services. And like many other businesses, this disjointed set of applications powered siloed, disconnected processes that led to inefficiencies, a poor customer experience, delayed quotes, and a lack of flexibility. On top of this the company experienced massive revenue leakage due to errors. The company's employees struggled to:

- Easily introduce and recommend new products, and third-party investment products
- Enable self-serve wealth and asset management
- Prevent rogue discounting

The Apttus solution enabled the organization to launch a collaborative, self-serve onboarding and wealth management portal featuring a rules-based asset and portfolio recommendation engine and approvals workflow. The portal provided the firm's wealth advisory managers with easy access to an automated quote and proposal generation solution that enabled its field sales staff to deliver completed proposals to financial advisors before leaving the advisors' offices. By doing so, they were able to implement self-service for a complex sales model where engaging and understanding the client is critical— and can even be considered the most important sales element. This dramatically improved the customer experience, while also reducing manual intervention and inefficiencies, and lowering plan administration costs and fees across the board.

## Be an Industry Mover and Shaker

Change is never easy and rarely welcomed. Corporate immune systems kick in. But the reality is that more than likely you need to make changes to your underlying processes if you want to see your business succeed in today's highly competitive, fast changing world. As these examples have shown, companies large and small across industries benefit from an automated Quote-to-Cash process. Whether they are focused on achieving back-office agility, driving omni-channel excellence, or realizing a customer-centric approach, they are succeeding with an integrated, automated Quote-to-Cash process. The benefit? Growing revenues, maintaining or improving margins, and eliminating business risk. And in many cases, they are positioning themselves as industry leaders.

# 8 Assessing Quote-to-Cash Maturity
## How Are You Doing?

**W**ith so many potential benefits to be realized by optimizing the end-to-end Quote-to-Cash process, it makes sense to benchmark where you may be in your process and execution maturity, so you can assess exactly what improvements and opportunities you may have to address. With this done, you will want to strive for as many improvements as possible so that you end up maximizing your business outcomes. A maturity model can be a tremendous tool to "sell" internally to gain buy in and a very good way to show how to take your company to the next level. That said, because of variations across businesses and industries, there are a number of maturity models that need to be thought through and used. No matter where you think you are in your Quote-to-Cash maturity, all organizations can improve the Quote-to-Cash process and we have seen endless evidence of this fact. When engaging with companies that run six sigma programs and have many professionally run programs in place, we still see very large opportunities to improve both revenue and the customer experience through improvements in Quote-to-Cash automation.

Assessing the maturity of a business process has become more common in the 21st century. In fact, an online search surfaces maturity models for a range of processes with one (major) gap: Quote-to-Cash. No established maturity model exists for Quote-to-Cash because it's a complex process spanning many business functions and sub-processes. Across industries, companies view these as a series of individual, disparate functions, which is part of the reason so many struggle to optimize their operations and revenues. When Quote-to-Cash is looked at as an integrated, end-to-end cycle, companies can gain many advantages. Apttus has developed a model that looks at the maturity of this critical operation.

The model allows companies to assess where they fall on their Quote-to-Cash maturity cycle and provides you with a plan to make progress. The model encompasses the four pillars that play into the success of any business process: strategy, people, process and technology.

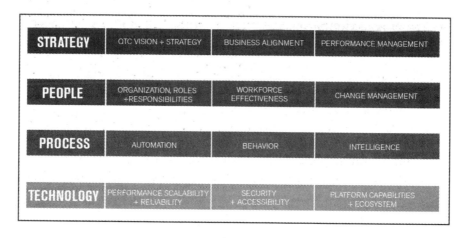

*Apttus Quote-to-Cash maturity model*

For the spectrum of Quote-to-Cash processes, the low end of maturity shows elementary use of standalone documents or spreadsheets, email-based workflows, and ad-hoc approvals. This leads to inconsistencies and inaccuracies, slowing down the overall Quote-to-Cash process. This threatens the company's ability to sell, win deals, fulfill orders and collect payments—ultimately affecting revenue and profitability.

The overarching goal of improving maturity in the Quote-to-Cash process is to drive better business outcomes and to do so as efficiently and effectively as possible. Let's walk through each of the four pillars that define Quote-to-Cash maturity and explore some of the underlying aspects in detail.

# Strategy

Within the Strategy pillar are these three sub-sections:

- Quote-to-Cash Vision & Strategy
- Business Alignment
- Performance Management

| STRATEGY | QTC VISION + STRATEGY | BUSINESS ALIGNMENT | PERFORMANCE MANAGEMENT |
|---|---|---|---|

## Quote-to-Cash Vision & Strategy

With the Quote-to-Cash process spanning so many business functions and no single person responsible for the overall process, it's essential that companies develop a Quote-to-Cash vision and strategy across the company. Most businesses lack these because there is no single owner until you reach the CFO or CEO.

An effective Quote-to-Cash process yields faster sales cycles, higher customer satisfaction, increased company growth, and improved profitability. These business benefits alone should be reason enough to develop a vision and solid strategy around Quote-to-Cash. Your vision is what you "imagine" you can achieve with an integrated Quote-to-Cash process, and your strategy is the plan to make that vision a reality and attain your business goals and outcomes.

This Quote-to-Cash maturity methodology will lay out a plan to improve the elements of specific business processes so that you can deliver on your strategy. Once your vision and strategy are formulated, you can define an operating model that will support—and allow all those involved to execute on—your Quote-to-Cash strategy.

Note that all effective Quote-to-Cash visions and strategies should be closely tied to your organization's overall business strategy.

An example: assume a company's strategy is to offer premium products to a discerning customer group who has many other competing options to choose from. It is therefore necessary to deliver an exceptional customer experience with the following attributes:

- Allow customers to research and order in any channel, and consume the service from anywhere they want
- Offer targeted products and promotions and deliver fast service to customers
- Enable seamless payments, and consider basing them on consumption-based billing

How does this translate to a Quote-to-Cash strategy? Here are some examples:

- The E-Commerce/omni-channel process needs to support product research and digital ordering, and be aligned with the direct sales force and channel partners
- Sales reps should be guided to suggest the most fitting product, and their compensation should be tied closely to configuring, pricing and quoting that product
- The order management/billing system must handle the complexity of subscription and usage-based invoicing

These might sound obvious, but this client was not thinking holistically across the Quote-to-Cash value chain and it was a surprise when all these elements came together for a complete strategy.

## Business Alignment

Once your company has defined its Quote-to-Cash vision and strategy, it's critical that the leadership team consistently makes decisions aligned with that strategy and that the Quote-to-Cash process is seamless and effective. This involves ensuring that all elements of Quote-to-Cash-related processes, which are embedded and prolific throughout the organization, conform to your company's strategic roadmap.

Consider a technology company selling a sophisticated piece of hardware. Just to configure the right product to meet the customer's needs, the sales team must involve the engineering team to confirm the configuration is accurate and realistic. At the same time, the supply chain/logistics team needs to confirm whether or not the delivery dates are reasonable, and the finance group has to approve pricing and confirm that it is aligned with the right promotions, etc. And those are just a few of the elements that go into the overall Quote-to-Cash process.

The decisions made across your organization should support the stated Quote-to-Cash strategy. For example, perhaps one goal is to more quickly respond to the marketplace. To that end, you need to make sure all decisions around a customer order contribute to a streamlined sales proposal. This may mean your company mandates fewer approval levels or focuses on approval by exception.

Hand in hand with this, your company needs to address all cross-functional areas when it outlines goals related to the Quote-to Cash strategy. Specifically, be sure to incent all functions to achieve the same objectives. As a simple example: marketing should not handle the launch or promotion of a new product in isolation. Marketing and your training group should enable and train the sales force on the new product, and sales management and the finance group should incent sellers to sell it.

Another example is the maintenance and rationalization of the product master. This exercise should take into account the intricacies of product configuration as well as the billing process.

## Performance Management

As is true of any good strategy and business operation, if you're not measuring how well you're doing, you're not really managing it. That's why it's important to measure how well your organization is performing when it comes to its Quote-to-Cash strategy.

By cascading your company's broad business objectives—or C-suite imperatives—down into actionable business drivers, you will identify metrics relating to the Quote-to-Cash process that you need to measure and manage. Take the example of a broad business goal like Revenue Growth. That goal can be correlated to Sales Efficiency and Sales Effectiveness goals for the VP of Sales. Those goals can then be tied to a Sales Velocity metric for each Regional Sales Director, and then further propagate down to Sales Cycle Speed for each Account Executive.

How do we tie this into the Quote-to-Cash process and related metrics? Proposal Drafting Speed and Quote Approval Speed are two metrics that influence overall Sales Cycle Speed. A streamlined, automated Quote-to-Cash process can improve the speed of those two activities. By measuring and managing each of these activities, the organization could reduce its overall sales cycle time. This would in turn lead to faster sales velocity. That would then help improve sales efficiency and effectiveness, which eventually help drive revenue growth. With an effective Quote-to-Cash process and solution in place, your organization could even tie compensation to these metrics to ensure that these two actions at the sales level are actually taking place.

# People

Within the People pillar are three sub-sections:

- Organization, Roles and Responsibilities
- Workforce Effectiveness
- Change Management

## Organization, roles and responsibilities

Your organization must be structured so that the Quote-to-Cash process can function in an integrated, seamless manner from end-to-end. At a high level, this means defining roles and responsibilities across the organization and ensuring that Quote-to-Cash activities are not performed in a vacuum but rather as part of a seamless, end-to-end process with a common goal. In a nutshell, this means that the right people must be in place across the organization to address every question that can arise and every decision that must be made from the time a quote is being put together until the revenue for that deal is recognized.

Consider the task of creating a quote. Perhaps the current process requires the quote to be reviewed and approved by eight people in different areas of the organization. Assessing the current process will probably identify redundancies. In this case, you determine that four of those eight people are simply going through a "rubber-stamping" exercise, while the other four are the ones who truly need to be involved in the approval. By removing those four from the process, quoting is greatly streamlined.

**Workforce effectiveness.** Here we are measuring the capabilities and skills of the workforce, as people are the ones who ultimately make the process work. Specifically, we measure how multi-functional and cross-dimensional skills are developed and rewarded, as needed, in a setting optimized for Quote-to-Cash. This touches upon everything from incentives and compensation to driving workforce effectiveness, to cultural issues such as institutionalizing rules and processes rather than trying to operate based on tribal knowledge.

**Change management.** Any business transformation requires change management. If your company is low on the Quote-to-Cash maturity model, lots will need to change in order for your process to progress up the maturity ladder. In addition to confirming your company's environment is conducive to change, it's advisable to conduct a comprehensive risk assessment, and make plans to address change resistance. Remember: no matter what technology a company purchases, if the underlying process is not well designed and adopted, nothing will change.

The fact is that companies can only achieve best-in-class Quote-to-Cash with seamless connections between every micro-process that goes into the overall process. This requires a commitment to a cohesive Quote-to-Cash process from all stakeholders, ranging from executives managing strategy to workers executing the elements. Accordingly, holding people accountable across all functional areas is paramount to a successful change.

# Process

When it comes to Quote-to-Cash, your organization needs to take a three-layered approach to drive measurable impact and positive business outcomes across the key sub-processes within the Quote-to-Cash area. These sub-processes include Configure-Price-Quote (CPQ), Contract Management, Order and Revenue Management, and Omni-Channel. The three "layers" are:

- Automation: more specifically, fully integrated Quote-to-Cash process automation to gain speed and efficiency

- Behavior: incenting and inspiring behaviors aligned with business objectives

- Intelligence: layering on system intelligence to provide guidance and provide users with information they did not know about so they can make a better decision

| PROCESS | AUTOMATION | BEHAVIOR | INTELLIGENCE |

To address the broad business challenges discussed earlier in the book, the first step is process automation. These are further improved through behavior change. Finally, they are optimized through layered-in intelligence. In other words, to achieve the best possible outcomes, your company must execute across all three "layers."

## Integrated Quote-to-Cash Process Automation

Companies achieve the first level of Quote-to-Cash maturity through process integration and automation that helps encourage and enable the right and best choices.

This lack of maturity manifests itself in:

- Inconsistent quoting, product promotions, and pricing
- Maverick discounting
- Inaccurate product configuration, available to promise dates and more
- Outdated contracts being used as ad-hoc templates
- The Legal team spends time rubber-stamping documents that don't need their attention
- Interested parties struggling to keep track of contract changes
- The contract process taking days or weeks
- Lower chance of winning business
- Slower response due to siloed systems

Moreover, with no analytics capabilities, no audit trail, governance, or compliance, your company has no visibility into contracts across its sales team and value chain.

If your contract management process isn't integrated within a full end-to-end Quote-to-Cash process, you are missing opportunities to streamline sales, standardize terms, increase efficiency and eliminate risk across the organization.

The following table shows examples of maturity indicators once a company has integrated and automated the various sub-processes within the Quote-to-Cash process.

| Maturity Indicators | | | |
|---|---|---|---|
| **CPQ** | **Contract Management** | **Order & Revenue Management** | **Omni-Channel** |
| Incentive compensation is aligned with the product sales, pricing, promotion strategies. | Individual business groups can initiate contracts, and request the contract types they need as well as time lines and urgency. Actionable reporting. | Ability to manipulate orders at the line level, see in-flight changes to orders, changing delivery conditions, and requirements. | Consistent products, prices, and promotions across channels and markets. |
| Accurate cost estimates and margin calculations on the fly during quoting. | Process occurs in near real time. Consistent legal language used across all contracts. Use of electronic signatures. All changes can be tracked in real time with visibility to all involved. | Asset-based ordering. Automatically pass all details captured in the quote to the contract and to finance team. | Efficient storefront, website, and catalog management. |
| Consistent, accurate pricing. | Ability to control and see whatever is necessary to improve compliance with government regulations. | Orders captured and consolidated across all channels including E-Commerce, distributors, partners, and direct sales. | Boost in E-Commerce transactions. |
| Full visibility into contracting, pricing and quoting across the value chain. | The business uses templates for everyday contracts and common clauses. Never miss a deadline or an obligation. | Order visibility for customers across channels, showing order status, including expected delivery dates, shipment costs, and taxes. | Increase in customer satisfaction. |
| Higher deal win rates, and average deal sizes. | High-value resources can focus on the exceptions. Changes to the contract are automatically delivered to teams. | Visibility and fulfillment across all channels. Reduction in inventory. On-time customer billing, accurate cash collections. | Decrease in sales cycle time. |
| Faster, more accurate quoting. | Centralized contracts with easy electronics access. | Fast intelligent renewals. | Increase in upsells /cross-sells. |

To achieve best-in-class order management, you need to integrate your Quote-to-Cash process with your CRM and ERP systems and any other back-office systems involved in inventory management, order fulfillment, service provisioning, and taxes. Additionally, you should be able to optimally orchestrate and fulfill orders using business rules and algorithms that can drive supply chain efficiency.

*Note: While we measure the discrete processes separately on the maturity scale, the ultimate goal is to integrate them within a single end-to-end process.*

When it comes to the first set of processes, the goal is to exert just enough control to ensure pricing within parameters, not putting wrong clauses in contracts, and other granular process automation elements.

Optimizing these Control-related processes is critical to ensuring good business outcomes.

## Changing behavior through incentives

The evolution from there is to change behavior. As was mentioned in chapter 4, maximizing your outcome or business objective requires deploying Quote-to-Cash Intelligence, which is not only about automating a process, but making sure the incentives for specific users involved in the process are aligned to drive the desired business outcome. When we say "users," we mean any person who is touching the business process, which can include any party involved in a business transaction. This includes your customers, partners and direct sales force in one of the following ways:

- **Promotions:** Marketing and promotions managers design, execute, manage and measure promotional campaigns across sales channels; your customers consume the promotion
- **Rebates:** Roll out, monitor and pay out rebates to your partners or end user customers
- **Commissions:** Calculate compensation and commission based on proposals and quotes created, and let your sales teams see the impact of their quotes on their earnings in real time; plan, manage and pay incentives to channel partners and resellers

Ultimately the goal is to encourage each party's behavior (channel, direct sales force, and customer) to be in alignment with your company's objectives, which may include the following:

- Increase revenue
- Promote cross-sell / upsell and increase overall deal size
- Retain and reward loyal customers
- Grow market share
- Attract new customers
- Provide marketing funds to channel partners
- Mask true price

Let's take the example of discounting without approval or maverick discounting. When it comes to maverick discounting, the automation goal would be to prevent a quote from being submitted for approval in the first place, by making the salesperson understand the consequence of doing so. This can be done by showing the salesperson that their compensation would be affected if they did submit for approval. The first step is to put in place a process for CPQ that helps put bounds around discounting. Unfortunately, the reality in many cases is that a salesperson will find ways to circumvent these restrictions. In that case, all the company has achieved is making the workforce use a different system; it is not changing behaviors and the outcome doesn't change.

To enact behavioral change, the company will need to provide incentives to the sales person. For instance, showing additional sales commission when a deal is not over-discounted. More than likely when sales reps see the upside in terms of their compensation, they will change their behavior. The same concept applies to any person touching the Quote-to-Cash process. For example, incenting third parties in the value chain, such as by providing partners with rebates and other incentives, to drive new and better behaviors, will also materially change the outcome.

When it comes to the Quote-to-Cash maturity scale, it's important to ensure that all incentives are covered and aligned.

- *Covered* means there is a solution/process in place that codifies the rebate, promotion, incentive, or channel rules and allows the organization to incentivize behavior in alignment with the organization's end goals. For example, promotions and rebates are used in different ways (e.g., on or off invoice, performance vs. non-performance based, etc.). One sign of maturity is to be able to handle—or cover— both promotions and rebates.

- Aligned means that incentives are in alignment. For instance, if the goal is to push certain products and bundles, the sales force's commission structure should incentivize the pushing of the associated promotions.

The following are examples of Quote-to-Cash maturity in this area:

| Incentive Process Maturity Indicators | |
|---|---|
| **Rebates** | **Promotions** |
| Supports multiple measurement types (Volume, Revenue, Market Share, Marketing Deliverable, Timely Submission, Growth) | Types (pull, push, performance-based, trials, tiered, buy-this-get-that) |
| Supports multiple benefit types (Fixed Amount, % or Per Unit, etc.) | Multiple benefit methods (amount off, discount, free duration/quantity, etc.) |
| Supports multiple entities (end customers, retailers, buying groups, wholesalers/distributors, etc.) | Multiple limit types (order specific, customer specific, time based, product based, etc.) |
| Supports a range of products (whole products, manufacturer/OEM SKUs, products with specific attributes, product family/hierarchy, etc.) | Cover multiple product types |
| Enables rebate accrual forecasting and visibility | Cover multiple channels |

## Going Beyond Automation

Some would say that once all stages of the end-to-end Quote-to-Cash process are being handled automatically and are working together seamlessly, companies have achieved full process maturity. But automation is only part of the solution. Companies must excel at addressing two additional layers beyond automation:

- Incentivizing/influencing behavior. This means defining the variables that go into decisions and putting bounds around potential end results.

- Providing advanced intelligence to make decisions. Here we are speaking of calling upon the intelligence of the system to guide optimal decisions.

## Layering in intelligence

The final rung on the rubric is to layer intelligence into the Quote-to-Cash system. Equipped with insights or information the user has never seen before, intelligence can provide guidance, drive behavior change, and deliver higher order value not previously achievable. This is done through machine learning. Machine learning has the benefit of access to a range of data that can shape informed, logical and insightful decisions. The data used for the insights can come from many sources including data in the end-to-end Quote-to-Cash process, existing market trends, ERP data, psychographic data, etc.

In the maverick discounting example, a Quote-to-Cash Intelligence system can recommend the optimal discount level depending on, for example, the customer's willingness to pay and the discount level required to win the business with a given win rate expectation.

We used maverick discounting to illustrate how a sophisticated Quote-to-Cash system and process supported by automation, behavioral influencers, and intelligence can improve sales-related process es. The same system can be used to exert control and change behavior across all areas of the Quote-to-Cash process. In fact, machine learning with access to real-time data inside the Quote-to-Cash system, is what enables a data-driven, Intelligent Quote-to-Cash process and moves companies up the maturity curve.

Machine learning in the form of Quote-to-Cash Intelligence enables organizations to truly understand customer and market dynamics. With this capability, organizations can "see around corners" and anticipate sales and buying trends, revenue at risk and new business opportunities. More importantly, they can exploit opportunities by taking informed, proactive measures (e.g., product bundling and cross-selling and upselling) that consistently improve their sales practices, customer relationships and therefore business outcomes.

## Gauging intelligence maturity

The intelligence layer also has a maturity scale as represented below.

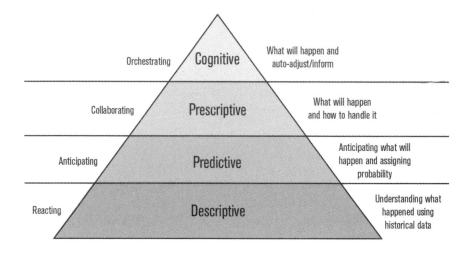

*Intelligence Capability Pyramid*

While many companies spend most of their time on descriptive analytics (what happened), true insight comes from diagnostic (why and how it happened) and predictive analytics (what will happen next).

**Descriptive analytics.** Descriptive analytics helps users understand what has already occurred. By laying out relevant summaries and supporting data in graphical formats, the data is easy to consume both by end-user staff and management.

*How can you use this type of analytics?* When it comes to pricing, a Quote-to-Cash Intelligence system can analyze your sell-side contracts and provide a report on customer pricing agreed to by different customer segments. Being equipped with this information will allow you to decide what pricing to offer in future deals of similar types. The system can also show other elements such as contracting terms and clauses that have been most successful in past deals. This allows you to decide which terms to include in the next authoring phase of a contract or which clauses need to be revisited by your team.

**Predictive analytics.** Predictive analytics helps users recognize patterns and detect meaningful trends. More significantly, it allows you to model projections over different time horizons based on the outcome you are looking for.

*How do you use this type of analytics?* For example, your Quote-to-Cash system can analyze successful deals, along with data mined from your lead database. When this is matched with a likely product rank, you'll be able to predict which of your prospects will likely buy, as well as which products they would likely buy. This allows you to plan your account priorities.

**Prescriptive analytics.** Prescriptive analytics delivers granular insights and forecasts showcasing what is likely to occur, accompanied by relevant, system-driven recommendations on next best actions and tactics to adopt.

*How can you use this type of analytics?* An example: If your Quote-to-Cash system tracks selling trends over an extended period of time, it will detect a spike in a particular product and provide certain recommendations. For instance, your system may tell you to allocate 25,000 extra units for a specific region, as opposed to the normal 15,000 you've been committed to in prior cases because of what it has seen in the data. This is a perfect example of proactively getting ahead of the curve to address rapidly changing needs of a customer.

**Cognitive analytics (machine driven).** Cognitive analytics uses machine learning to mine data and therefore refine trend and pattern analyses on an on-going, unsupervised basis. The machine constantly evaluates processes and other related data. It can lead to automatically initiating specific, suitable actions and workflows.

*How can you use this type of analytics?* An example: Your Quote-to-Cash system detects an increase in demand for a product in a certain region and therefore automatically adjusts the price slightly to match demand, generating a greater profit. No more manual work to derive valuable insights. No more missed opportunities. Instead, your company can take action at the speed needed to be competitive.

Ultimately, these intelligent, data-driven insights will help organizations sell smarter by leveraging the data at their disposal to drive productive change within their processes. Intelligent Quote-to-Cash is being developed to provide insights that are not only cognitive and predictive, but also prescriptive, providing data-based recommendations that drive smarter business decisions and results.

The ultimate goal is to move up the maturity scale. This can be done when using data, as opposed to "gut" reactions, to create quotes and contracts by automatically adjusting terms that result in a better outcome.

# Technology

Once you have strategy and the right people and processes in place, technology is the enabler of your optimized Quote-to-Cash process. The ideal system needs to address the following items at minimum, as indicated within the Technology pillar of the maturity model:

- Performance, Scalability & Reliability
  - Performance (includes transaction capacity, response times, latency, etc.)
  - Scalability (includes linear transactional performance, scale up and out, etc.)
- Reliability (includes high availability, redundancy, disaster recovery, etc.)
- Security & Accessibility
  - Security & Compliance (for example, Sarbanes-Oxley)
  - Accessibility (covers global footprint, mobile access, customer/partner access, field sales access)
- Platform Capabilities & Ecosystem
  - Flexibility, interoperability, and integration capabilities

- ◆ Ecosystem (includes development community, developer tools, SDKs, applications, support)

- ◆ Innovative (platform partner, continued investment and innovation in platform, analytics capabilities, etc.)

- ◆ Cost (low operational total cost of ownership through, for example, pay for computation/storage use only)

As we have previously discussed, if you use a single platform to support the Quote-to-Cash process, it provides a single source of truth. This is critical for driving the most value possible from the Quote-to-Cash process. But it is very difficult to achieve—if not impossible—when integrating multiple, disparate solutions deployed within and managed by different departments.

## Measuring Progress on the Maturity Scale

Definitions of each stage on the Quote-to-Cash process maturity scale are shown below:

- Awareness—Company is still relying on an ad hoc, manual, disconnected and resource-intensive process fraught with errors and accuracy issues.

- Developing—Company has automated and integrated some internal aspects of the Quote-to-Cash process. With control through automation of processes, the company sees a faster, more accurate Quote-to-Cash process.

- Competitive—Company has automated and integrated some internal and external aspects of the Quote-to-Cash process. This manifests itself in a more efficient and effective sales force (including channel partners), and bigger deal sizes.

- Leading—Company is operating on a fully integrated, automated Quote-to-Cash process supported by behavioral and intelligence influencers, leading to competitive advantage and the ability to impact win rates, revenue, profitability and more. This is the nirvana of Quote-to-Cash and allows the company to drive topline growth in a number of ways.

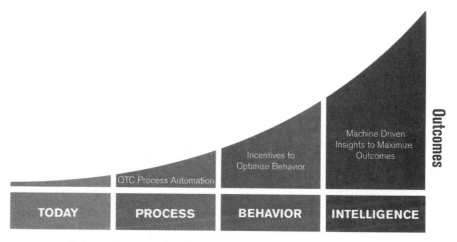

*Advancing up the Quote-to-Cash maturity spectrum leads to better business outcomes*

In summary: To move up the maturity scale, your company needs to address all four pillars of the maturity framework: automating processes, changing behavior and layering in intelligence.

Ultimately your company can determine its progress on the maturity scale by asking: Are we quoting and contracting with a high level of accuracy, speed, and visibility? Moreover, are we providing the right information or intelligence at the right time to make the best possible decisions? And are we doing so seamlessly across all functions, in a way that aligns desired business outcomes with our sales team, customer, and partner behaviors?

If so, you have become a world class organization.

# 9 Capitalizing on the Potential ROI of Quote-to-Cash Automation

**A**s we have seen in previous chapters, deploying an automated, integrated Quote-to-Cash process, your company can achieve very significant financial, operational and customer benefits. But what is the true ROI of automating the Quote-to-Cash process? Because Quote-to-Cash is a revenue process, any improvements usually yield very large financial gains and therefore high ROI. It is not difficult to quickly establish and realize ROI by improving your Quote-to-Cash process. The improvement of ROI comes from your organization and its operations across the entire spectrum of your business. Quote-to-Cash automation gives you a single view of customer-related transactions, contractual "gives and gets," invoices (what you've billed) and revenue schedules (what you've been paid). In other words, it provides a single, unified data model to run your business—a promise that CRM tools have been making for many years and yet no one has delivered on it. Now you can, with an ROI that is large and real.

When underpinning the generic Quote-to-Cash process with machine learning and artificial intelligence, the process improves even more dramatically, achieving even greater ROI. By implementing a simple process automation tool with a deeply insightful artificial intelligence machine learning tool, you can create a huge competitive advantage for the organization. How? Instead of just reading reports about what's happened, managers across your organization are presented with intelligence that highlights good, better and best outcomes. This enables you to satisfy everything from C-level imperatives such as increased growth, market share and profitability to line-of-business goals such as faster sales velocity, fewer contracting mistakes, and better order and invoice accuracy.

Quote-to-Cash ROI is measured in financial and non-financial (i.e., productivity) terms. These metrics and KPIs include:

**Financial**

- Sales and sales promotion achievement
- Revenue and channel growth
- Revenue targets for cross-sell and up-sell growth
- Margin Improvement
- Renewal rate and account growth
- Quota achievement and incentive compensation payout
- Financial risk reduction

**Productivity**

- Quoting productivity including speed, accuracy, and compliance
- Sales conversion and product and service attach rates
- Customer retention rates
- Operational cycle times
- Forecast accuracy
- Error reduction (e.g., misquoting, missed delivery dates)

Let's walk through the impact of an optimized Quote-to-Cash process across your organization.

## Accelerate the sales cycle and increase revenues

With an optimized Intelligent Quote-to-Cash process, Sales can improve in many areas:

*Achieve the maximum potential with each customer sale by making quoting decisions based on key metrics. Some examples:*

- **Customer propensity to buy** (i.e., the products and services most likely to be purchased by your customer). Even without an integrated Quote-to-Cash process, your Sales group can unearth patterns of products/services sold to certain customer types. For example, "In Europe, customers prefer X, Y, Z." But when dealing with a large product catalog, and accounting for sales through different channels and a combination of numerous deal characteristics, it's challenging—if not impossible—for a human to spot these trends. At the same time, someone can easily overlook a subtle indication of customer needs and products/services of value. But with an integrated Intelligent Quote-to-Cash process and end-to-end visibility across the value chain, machine learning can uncover opportunities such as "At renewal, lots of SMB customers are attempting to move to next maturity stage and need this type of support package." Or "We see many SMBs signing up for this support level." Having the sales person presented with this insight can dramatically improve your sales and revenue and therefore ROI.

- **The best offering for your customer.** Quote-to-Cash automation allows you to track gross and net margin by deal, product line and individual customer. This data can provide an edge when your company is developing new products and setting prices for both new and existing product lines. Want to compare each deal to the best deals? This level of granularity on margin is more insightful than gross margin because it includes the total costs associated with making a sale (e.g., cost to serve and cost to fulfill). This metric lets you determine which deals put more cash in your pocket and are the best deals. Analyzing these margins can surface operating issues in contracting and fulfillment that stem from incorrect configurations, challenging delivery schedules or poorly written or enforced terms and conditions.

## Redefine the sales process

An automated, integrated Quote-to-Cash process ensures your Sales team is protected with guardrails. Ensure quotes contain accurate product information, deals comply with pricing and discounting rules down to individual line items, and the necessary approvals are gathered quickly without slowing down deals.

*Introduce segment-specific prices and increase the responsiveness of changes in pricing and discounts.*

It's sometimes necessary to discount in order to win business. But discounting should be done in a strategic way and managed closely. An integrated Quote-to-Cash process provides visibility to sales reps into discount thresholds and the level of approval necessary when thresholds are exceeded. If a discount is sought, Sales leadership is notified if the discount exceeds predetermined thresholds and they can approve these in strategic situations. Your C-level team sees how pricing is adding to the top and bottom line with discounting trends and how pricing and discounts are impacting company-wide margins. With this level of visibility and control, your company can turn discounting from a necessary evil into a smart strategic lever to win business while staying profitable.

*Understand which incentives and add-ons drive the highest propensity for customer purchase and maximize deal value by tracking and monitoring these metrics:*

- **Promotional performance.** With the data supplied from an integrated Quote-to-Cash process, you can pinpoint which promotions are producing incremental sales or driving incremental margin dollars. For example, when a discount is extended, do we win incremental sales or deals without sacrificing pricing power or profitability?

- **Price realization / pricing performance.** Determining where and when to use pricing power is a struggle for many enterprises. Are you able to say with certainty that your company's prices are moving upward, holding steady or declining? Knowing where you have pricing power and measuring the impact of pricing actions is key. But this is especially challenging when managing a catalog of thousands of items and working with an ecosystem of partners and channels around the world.

- **Maverick pricing.** When it comes to allowing Sales to extend discounts, companies should aim for a balance of control and speed. On the one end, your company could enable Sales to choose prices so they can get quotes to the customer quickly. But your organization will likely soon feel as though quoting is out of control. At the other end, too much oversight and supervision on quotes and discounts grinds the pace of Sales to a halt. In other words, neither option is optimal.

With an integrated Quote-to-Cash process powered by the right system, your company can apply controls without giving up speed. More specifically, it can steer Sales reps and other users to make decisions that are good for the customer, good for your company and good for the Sales rep. The right system does this by giving pricing guidance to Sales reps and backing recommendations with incentives so the rep sees the impact of a certain pricing choice.

## Boost channel impact

An automated, integrated Quote-to-Cash process drives the success of your global, omni-channel selling strategy by ensuring:

- All channels are always operating off the same, current product and pricing information

- You can manage revenue-share programs, channel exclusive discounts, and location-based pricing and shipping fees

- Full visibility into sales trends for each channel, so your executives can course-correct when needed

- Channel consistency so customers can find the same product everywhere you offer it, and at prices you control, making it easy to do business with you while allowing you to drive maximum value from all of your channels

### See which customers are up for renewal

By easily seeing which customers are renewing, Sales can strategically plan to expand a relationship or further penetrate an account. Because an integrated Quote-to-Cash process automatically tracks contract expiration dates and generates an opportunity record for the appropriate Sales rep, your company can address renewals early and strategically. Additionally, with a single repository of contract-related data, your organization can easily see which customers are targets for cross-sell and up-sell.

### Increase sales velocity

Moving deals through the pipeline more quickly is the goal of every Sales organization. Here's what the Sales Velocity Factor looks like:

Sales Velocity Factor = [(# of opportunities) * (average deal size) * (win rate)] / (sales cycle time)

You can improve each of the formula dimensions through an integrated Quote-to-Cash process. With automated, standardized quotes and contracts, your Sales reps can generate quotes faster, within approval guidelines, and your managers can approve them more quickly when additional approvals are necessary.

At the same time, extending your Quote-to-Cash process to span your entire value chain makes it possible for your company to enable the channel in support of more opportunities. This in turn allows your business to address more pipeline, close more opportunities and boost its win rate. If you operate on a subscription-based revenue model—which is increasingly important to businesses of all types—faster close will also often lead to higher first-year revenue for a new account. At the same time, with insight into which product bundles and add-ons are likely to appeal to a certain customer, your Sales team can increase deal sizes.

Advanced, Quote-to-Cash Intelligence systems offer advantages because they provide a single source of truth that extends your CRM (customer relationship management) system. For instance, Apttus can pull past purchase history, order volumes, order frequencies and other details from a CRM tool and feed it into the Apttus E-Commerce solution. From there, the system can apply advanced analytics and Quote-to-Cash Intelligence to make product, upsell/cross-sell, and pricing recommendations. Your company can even leverage Apttus to gain traction for promotions and rebates across its ecosystem of resellers and distributors.

### Improve E-Commerce results

- **Average order value.** If your company is making use of an E-Commerce solution and gathering data around average order sizes for both direct sales and partner sales, it can use an integrated Quote-to-Cash process to evaluate ways to boost this by various means. This can include intelligent product bundling, cross-selling, and upselling.

- **Customer churn.** It's a given that you want to reduce customer churn. With Intelligent Quote-to-Cash and an advanced E-Commerce solution, you can present the right products at the right price to encourage additional purchases, ensure a seamless checkout process, and deliver a differentiated customer experience.

- **Customer lifetime value.** An optimized Quote-to-Cash process paired with a robust E-Commerce solution can dramatically improve the amount of revenues you'll generate over a customer's lifetime. While the E-Commerce solution leverages promotions, rebates, and more, the quoting engine enables a self-service process online including contracting right through the contract close using e-Signatures. Together, these technologies enable a seamless, low-friction experience for customers, boosting the likelihood of repeat purchases.

- **Conversion rate.** With advanced E-Commerce capabilities, your company can track the number of site visitors that purchase using a shopping cart, as well as attach rates and abandonment rates. Moreover, it can see how partners are using the portal, such as for opportunity logging, quoting, service delivery, and support. All of these insights enable your company to make adjustments to improve partner performance and conversion rates.

## Reduce risk without slowing down business

With comprehensive visibility and foresight around expectations and instructions for both parties captured in contracts, your Legal team can use the data in contracts to empower faster contracting using standardized templates. Your Sales reps and Legal team will be happier and, importantly, they will have more time to dedicate to the large, needle-moving deals that require handholding and exceptions. Additionally, you'll have a better handle on deal-related legal and financial risks. This is a huge benefit because your organization can now forecast and plan with more precision.

## Legal

With an optimized Quote-to-Cash process, Legal can:

### *Drive more favorable deals by flowing up-to-date Legal language from quotes to contracts*

The Sales contract is the document that defines the value being delivered to the customer and your firm's incentive to deliver. In other words, it outlines the terms of your trading relationship over the life of the relationship. An Intelligent Quote-to-Cash process can leverage the insights from past contracts to produce the best contract results efficiently and quickly. This helps your organization get to revenue as quickly as possible.

An integrated Quote-to-Cash process allows your company to extend machine learning guidance to the contracting stage. Specifically, Legal can define the terms that will put your organization in the best possible position to create and deliver value while retaining its fair share. This leads to deals that fairly compensate your company and keep it incented to deliver, which in turn provides you with money to reinvest.

### Contracts are the roadmap to business deals

Contracts determine what someone is paying you, how long they'll be paying you, any services or support or re-work you are responsible for—and for how long you're responsible. They also indicate the terms for renewal, and when and how the customer can terminate. Any mistakes in the contract process can increase your liability and significantly impact your bottom line.

## When contracts go bad

Common contract issues that can be avoided with an integrated, automated Quote-to-Cash process:

- Your company is normally paid within 30 days but agrees to 75- or 90-day terms. This puts additional costs on your organization, whether material or productivity-related.

- Your company commits to delivering technology ahead of its roadmap. To satisfy this, it will incur expenses for talent to accelerate the development timeline. Additionally, if your organization misses the timeline, you might be penalized for not meeting the SLA.

- Your company gets into a disagreement with a customer about a term in the contract or delivered per the contract. This leads to litigation and legal costs.

### *Control and standardize contract language*

Avoiding free-typed, deal-specific, unapproved contract language ensures the best risk-reward profile for both your business and your customers. By using contract templates and pre-written conditional clauses supported by an automated Quote-to-Cash process, your company gains both flexibility and control when generating contract language. A template written and approved by your Legal department ensures that language does not put your company at risk and that it can deliver on these promises both profitably and with high customer satisfaction. While pre-written conditional clauses may require certain approvals, they help ensure that variances are controlled and that associated risks are understood.

### *Score agreements/deals based on risk profile*

Your Legal team tries to provide controls and mitigate risk in the most efficient manner and doesn't want to slow down sales process more than necessary. At the same time, your Sales reps don't want to be surprised by roadblocks in contracts. Let Sales do what it does best—close the deal rapidly. With an integrated Quote-to-Cash process, your Legal team can mitigate and engineer risk out of the system. In fact, by calling upon machine intelligence, it can identify and avoid risks and the downstream costs associated with them. In other words, it can create a relatively hands-free environment with controls your firm needs without inhibiting growth.

## Overcome the Speed vs. Control Conundrum

The biggest source of friction, when it comes to sales contracts, comes from the balancing act between speed and control. Because contracts are so critical, Legal's preference is to be diligent and therefore move more slowly, to examine contracts discerningly. Sales is often a major antagonist to such thoroughness, pressuring Legal to get out of the way so deals can be closed faster. With an integrated, automated Quote-to-Cash process, contracts can move through quickly but with enough oversight to effectively mitigate risk.

### *Appropriately allocate resources*

You want the right people working on the right tasks when it comes to contracts. Your experienced, expensive and knowledgeable employees should work on needle-moving deals representing big financial gains. With an integrated Quote-to-Cash process, Legal can work off standard agreements and terms (rather than deal with non-standard terms and conditions inserted by Sales reps) wherever possible. This makes the process as self-service and automated as possible for Sales on standard deals. It also allows them to focus less on transactional, repetitive activities and more on strategic, value-added initiatives.

## Optimize business results

Revenue management is everything that occurs after a contract is signed, from invoicing, billing and order management to rebate programs and revenue recognition. This aspect of the Quote-to-Cash process is critical to accurately and efficiently realizing revenue. While Finance carries out many of the revenue management tasks, the outcomes of revenue management impact a variety of departments—from Sales and Marketing to Finance and Legal.

When done right, revenue management enables your company to manage multiple revenue model structures—one-time, recurring revenue streams and subscriptions, and hybrid bundles of the two—for different lines of business, even as contract values change over time. This enables your organization to be more consistent across channels, more customer-friendly, and more efficient once deals are signed.

To make revenue management as seamless as possible, it's important to integrate this function with sales, contracts and order fulfillment data. This enables your Finance team to track details all the way through to entry in the general ledger and enables your company to keep an accurate record of the value it has earned from each deal.

## Finance

With an optimized Quote-to-Cash process, Finance can:

### *Recognize revenue faster and more accurately*

Forecasts are historically made based on closed deals. With an integrated Quote-to-Cash process, single data model and the ability to mine intelligent insights, your organization can include additional richness in its forecasts. In other words, you can look further ahead to understand deals in the pipeline and score the deals with a confidence rating based on understanding customer and deal attributes—for example, "this deal has a high certainty of closing." We're not suggesting your organization move away from the norm when it comes to forecasting. But we do want to recognize that an integrated Quote-to-Cash process and a single data model provides more context and confidence about forecasts. That allows decisions to be based on the most relevant information.

## Improve billing and invoicing accuracy

There is always the risk that under billing will result in lost revenue while over billing will result in delayed revenue (from time-consuming adjustments) and therefore dissatisfied customers. Billing can also very quickly become complicated: your company might have multiple contracts with a single customer, it might bill for one-time items as well as subscription services, and it might offer tiered pricing or rebates. Like many companies, yours might also have a contractual right to increase pricing each year as indexed to inflation.

It is a time-consuming and error-prone process to manage all these revenue streams and price changes accurately and bill for them the way a customer requests. With an integrated Quote-to-Cash process, your Finance team has access to accurate data about quotes and contracts. Surfacing accurate cost and usage data on a customer to the billing department goes a long way to improving accuracy and stemming revenue leakage. And that means your organization can issue more accurate invoices and do so more quickly.

### Why traditional back-office systems won't cut it

While enterprise resource planning (ERP), financial systems and operational systems help execute back-end processes and track transactions efficiently, the lack of flexibility makes it difficult for customers and partners to do business. Rigid systems can't accommodate rapidly changing business models. Often they require extensive integration to accommodate last minute-changes that come from more customer-facing systems like CRM. Even worse, companies lack a single view of the customer and partner when relying on these systems.

## Marketing

With an optimized Quote-to-Cash process, Marketing can improve the following:

- **Product attach rate.** With insight into how much new product your company is selling and whether or not the new product is displacing old ones, Marketing can take measures to encourage faster uptake on new products.

- **Product portfolio management.** With an integrated Quote-to-Cash process, your pricing analysts and product teams can easily see how much money your company is making on new, mature, and sunset products. They can also easily see how revenue and margin changes over time. An advanced Quote-to-Cash system can deliver intelligence to sales teams in the quoting and renewal process. As a result, your company can effectively manage the yield on your product lifecycle and avoid the pitfalls of errors, dead ends, and excessive warranty cost associated with end-of-life products and product catalog evolution sunset replacements.

## Operations

With an optimized Quote-to-Cash process, Operations can improve:

- **Order fulfillment.** To optimize order fulfillment and delivery, your Operations team needs insight into a breadth of activity: by volume, geography, cycle time of orders, and where and when the order fulfillment process is likely to break down and why. With an integrated Quote-to-Cash process, it can easily see the number of orders and how they break out. This allows your team to make the smartest choices ahead of time for filling those orders on time as efficiently as possible.

- **Error reduction.** The perfect order (and perfect invoice) flows from the perfect quote. With an Intelligent Quote-to-Cash process, you greatly reduce or altogether eliminate snags from misquoting, contract and invoice errors, and missed delivery dates stemming from mistakes.

- **Inventory management.** Your Operations team makes decisions about what inventory to carry based on forecasted orders. With an integrated Quote-to-Cash process, supply and demand details would be connected, allowing Operations to stay abreast of the latest forecasts and inventory requirements. At the same time, Sales can easily see when there's an inventory shortfall, and avoid making promises that can't be kept.

## Run the business smartly

Because the Quote-to-Cash process lies at the very heart of your business, it's critical for your executives to have a full view into all inputs and outputs from the process. This empowers them to call upon precision insights when making strategic decisions that impact your company's current and future state.

With an optimized Quote-to-Cash process, your executives can:

*Gain the visibility to confidently assess revenue flow, and ensure the business is running effectively.*

If Quote-to-Cash is a series of disjointed processes with data being stored in multiple systems, company decisions, strategic planning, and investments may be poorly informed or worse. For instance, your executives may decide to move forward with an investment based on cash flow only to find out that issues in the customer base are resulting in reduced renewals rates. And that will have a material impact on future cash flows. An integrated Quote-to-Cash process puts all the information you need in a standard format in one place, calling upon a single data model and single data source. As a result, everyone is working off the same understanding of your company's position and where it's headed. In other words, a single view of the customer.

With the right data, your executive team can answer important questions, such as:

- Which customer segments are growing?
- Which product groups are growing?

- Which partners are most valuable to us and in which ways?
- How can we grow customer accounts by analyzing historical performance?
- What are the best options to grow average deal size and margins over time?
- What are the risks to revenue in our business?
- How can we improve our ability to serve our customers?

Informed by a more robust understanding of business, sales, and pipeline of future business, your C-suite gets a better picture of commercial operations and revenue.

## The value of integrated Quote-To-Cash

When Quote-to-Cash is a disconnected series of events, it's nearly impossible to measure any single stage or piece together the sequence of customer touches. With a single process and data model for the Quote-to-Cash process, your company can easily and accurately measure effectiveness across the entire process, and take steps to optimize it. By reducing cycle time, your company more quickly achieves higher revenue. Also, you're freeing workers' time to do more productive work like creating more quotes. With more time to understand your customers' needs and with guidance on which offerings would best satisfy those and your company's goals, your sales reps can also increase the size of their deals

## The Future of Quote-to-Cash

We have entered an age in which we will increasingly rely on intelligent assistants to help us achieve more. This will free us up from unnecessary activities in order to do work that is uniquely suited to our particular abilities. The changes will be dramatic. Productivity soars. And satisfaction improves dramatically.

Today, those same powerful intelligent assistants are helping us explore new worlds and assuming mundane activities like driving and deliveries.

We don't have to look too far down the road to see when machine-to-machine interaction will eliminate mistakes and further streamline value exchange in the Quote-to-Cash process. We are entering the era of driverless applications.

In the future, machine interaction will allow us to better navigate the business landscape. To see around corners with clarity and precision. And anticipate and prepare for an unknown horizon.

Access to integrated Quote-to-Cash data enables your company to make tremendous progress in achieving its strategic goals. But the next generation of integrated Quote-to-Cash Intelligence solutions will go a step beyond. Cognitive machine intelligence is powering advanced Quote-to-Cash solutions that guide users to take actions that increase productivity in all business functions. This optimizes results for companies. Imagine for a moment the Quote-to-Cash system identifying trends and providing a recommendation to invest in a new line of business or a merger or acquisition strategy. The system would then guide senior managers through an assessment of the strategy and the most likely scenarios to achieve the desired business results.

Next-generation Quote-to-Cash isn't about waiting for product management to refresh product lines, but instead is telling product marketing what new bundles to create, telling R&D what new product lines to develop, adjust discounts and optimize pricing in real time by customer and industry. In other words, the essence of Quote-to-Cash Intelligence is about giving companies choices to contemplate so they can increase the likelihood of reaching their strategic goals. This is accomplished through a sophisticated Intelligent Quote-to-Cash system that can guide user behavior while empowering them with intelligence.

## Enabling touchless sales

Quote-to-Cash Intelligence systems ultimately will enable touchless (or frictionless) sales. An integrated, automated Quote-to-Cash process featuring sanctioned quote and contract templates and intelligent guidance empowers, sales reps to assemble and price optimal deals on their own, from any location at any time.

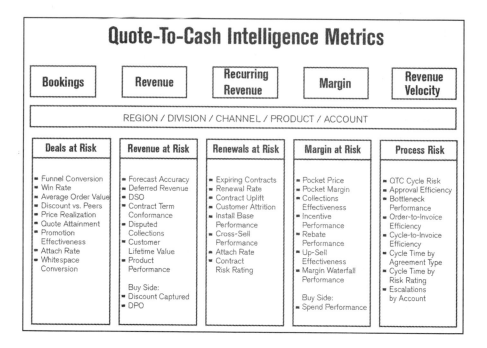

# Quote-To-Cash Intelligence Metrics

| Bookings | Revenue | Recurring Revenue | Margin | Revenue Velocity |
|---|---|---|---|---|

REGION / DIVISION / CHANNEL / PRODUCT / ACCOUNT

| Deals at Risk | Revenue at Risk | Renewals at Risk | Margin at Risk | Process Risk |
|---|---|---|---|---|
| ■ Funnel Conversion<br>■ Win Rate<br>■ Average Order Value<br>■ Discount vs. Peers<br>■ Price Realization<br>■ Quote Attainment<br>■ Promotion Effectiveness<br>■ Attach Rate<br>■ Whitespace Conversion | ■ Forecast Accuracy<br>■ Deferred Revenue<br>■ DSO<br>■ Contract Term Conformance<br>■ Disputed Collections<br>■ Customer Lifetime Value<br>■ Product Performance<br><br>Buy Side:<br>■ Discount Captured<br>■ DPO | ■ Expiring Contracts<br>■ Renewal Rate<br>■ Contract Uplift<br>■ Customer Attrition<br>■ Install Base Performance<br>■ Cross-Sell Performance<br>■ Attach Rate<br>■ Contract Risk Rating | ■ Pocket Price<br>■ Pocket Margin<br>■ Collections Effectiveness<br>■ Incentive Performance<br>■ Rebate Performance<br>■ Up-Sell Effectiveness<br>■ Margin Waterfall Performance<br><br>Buy Side:<br>■ Spend Performance | ■ QTC Cycle Risk<br>■ Approval Efficiency<br>■ Bottleneck Performance<br>■ Order-to-Invoice Efficiency<br>■ Cycle-to-Invoice Efficiency<br>■ Cycle Time by Agreement Type<br>■ Cycle Time by Risk Rating<br>■ Escalations by Account |

# Conclusion:
# The Time is Now to Revolutionize
# Your Quote-to-Cash Process

Achieving strategic business outcomes in today's business environment is anything but easy. Most businesses are dealing with, more buying and selling channels (and extended value chains), more business and pricing model pressure, more global competition and commoditization, more market volatility, and more regulations. Complicating matters, the classic—static—selling and distribution model is simply not designed to support the demands and preferences of today's more discerning buyers. Consumers today traverse multiple channels including web, social, mobile and even virtual to research, purchase, and use products and services. Customers want the power to purchase how and when they want.

To adapt and be successful in this new environment, your organization must be customer-centric across its business. This means your organization must be available to customers in any channel of their choice (i.e., be omni-channel). It also means your business needs to be designed to interact and transact with customers as quickly—and accurately—as possible.

Therefore, more and more businesses are adopting digitally enabled channels, including E-Commerce: these channels make the customer engagement process easy, whether customers are making their first purchase or repeat purchases. And a smoother buying process translates into a company that customers enjoy doing business with.

But that's not enough. Your company must also enable different business functions and parties in the extended value chain—whether suppliers, partners, OEMs or others—to plan, monitor, and respond simultaneously. You need to enable the entire value chains of separate companies to act as a single, contiguous entity sharing insight and intelligence.

In other words, your company must ensure a continuum of interactions and a seamless customer experience across channels and throughout the value chain. Yet few organizations have been able to coordinate omni-channel efforts to maximize the customer experience.

Quote-to-Cash is the business process that sits right underneath the customer success process. Therefore, effectively automating and managing Quote-to-Cash becomes critical to the success of a company's interactions with its customers. But today Quote-to-Cash is dramatically sub-optimized. One key reason is the continued reliance on separate, siloed systems to enable the Quote-to-Cash process. This leads to inconsistent data about customers and orders, which in turn leads to mistakes and confusion that hamper attempts to deliver a smooth customer experience. All this translates into lost sales and customers.

The ability to accommodate buyers' needs in today's digital landscape—and across the extended value chain—requires more than a simple tweaking of your company's internal processes. It requires total transformation of the way you go from Quote-to-Cash.

But even that isn't enough. You must do more than automate the process of Quote-to-Cash. You also need to harness enterprise applications to understand the motivations of each of the players across the process and ensure that they are being incented in the right way to drive a desired outcome. It doesn't matter if you want the outcome to be that a certain product is recommended, a certain price is proposed, or something else. You cannot influence that outcome unless you provide your employees, partners and others—i.e., those involved in the Quote-to-Cash process—with an incentive that makes them change behavior to achieve your desired outcome. Behavior-based applications motivate your company to focus on a common goal and therefore achieve a better outcome.

Additionally, invariably somewhere in your organization there is data or information that can help a user in the Quote-to-Cash process to make a better decision. So it's imperative that a system can call upon all the data collected across the organization to feed new information and insights to those involved in the Quote-to-Cash process. This is called *Intelligent* Quote-to-Cash. It uses machine learning and artificial intelligence to dramatically increases the value of that data and of the actions taken by everyone involved in the process. Intelligent Quote-to-Cash delivers a substantially better outcome for the company and your customers.

The Apttus Intelligent Cloud has fundamentally changed the way enterprise applications work today. First, it enables your company to move to the front office, many of the activities and processes traditionally relegated to the back office. This means that customers can access much more relevant information more quickly, truly helping them realize a more satisfactory experience with your company. But more importantly, it combines process-based applications with behavior-based applications and machine learning to substantially improve business outcomes. As users perform actions, the Cloud interprets data (and learns over time) to feed users with insights they can apply to choose the best possible outcome for your company and its customers.

Quote-to-Cash Intelligence strategies enabled with scalable, secure and globally available cloud platforms, empower your organization to inject its innate intelligence and knowledge into every sales situation. While on-premise systems can also help do this, cloud-based ones are quicker to roll out, easier to customize, and often more rapidly and widely adopted by those in the extended value chain. Integrated, cloud-based, Intelligent Quote-to-Cash allows your company to fluidly connect its critical data and processes. And that means any party within the value chain is empowered to accurately and quickly move deals through the pipeline from opportunity to close.

It's critical that your company prioritize the modernization of its core processes in response to the many shifts shaping today's business landscape. A disjointed Quote-to-Cash process actually undermines efforts to drive the best business outcomes. It's impossible to close deals as quickly as possible, ensure the most favorable contract terms, go above and beyond the call to satisfy customers, and record profitable revenues without an integrated, automated Intelligent Quote-to-Cash process. In fact, it's not possible to launch and support the new business models and extended value chains required to succeed in today's global economy without a seamless Quote-to-Cash process.

But an automated, integrated, Quote-to-Cash process in the cloud—fueled with machine learning and intelligence—empowers your company to achieve measurable financial and operational benefits. This optimized process makes it possible to improve business across the board, everything from marketing to fulfillment.

Numerous companies across industries have already crossed the chasm, and modernized their Quote-to-Cash process with these intelligence-fueled applications that impact and shape behavior. That means you don't need to break new ground in pursuing this transformation: you simply have to follow in the footsteps of those that have already succeeded by doing so.

We have even provided a maturity model so your organization can assess where it falls on the Quote-to-Cash maturity scale and therefore generate a plan to improve your capabilities. In other words, you have everything you need to bring order to the current chaos that is preventing your company from achieving its full potential. Now it's time for you to lead the charge for true and meaningful business transformation and make your entire organization easy to do business with.

As we say at Apttus, be careful when implementing a Quote-to-Cash Intelligence system—you may sell too much!

# About the Author

Kirk Krappe is a veteran of Enterprise Software with over two decades of SaaS experience and an E&Y Entrepreneur of the Year Finalist, having been involved in the very first instances of online enterprise applications. Kirk has extensive experience marketing, selling and delivering enterprise solutions to organizations worldwide.

In 2006, Kirk co-founded the SaaS company, Apttus. Apttus is the category-defining Quote-to-Cash software company that drives the vital business process between the buyer's interest in a purchase and the realization of revenue. Applications include Configure-Price-Quote (CPQ), Renewals, Contract Management, Revenue Management and E-Commerce. Today, under Kirk's leadership as CEO the company has over 500 customers, offices in several countries and multiple patents pending.

Previous to Apttus, Kirk held the role of Executive Vice President of Worldwide Markets at iMANY. Additionally, Kirk was Chief Executive Officer of Nextance, a privately-held contract management solutions provider. Kirk was also Senior Vice President at Corio through Corio's initial public offering where he pioneered the original concept of SaaS before it became mainstream. Kirk also served as Vice President of Solutions Marketing with Oracle and Vice President of Industry Solutions with Siebel Systems. Kirk has an Electrical and Mechanical Engineering Degree from the University of London and an MBA from INSEAD, Europe's leading business school.